3̲0̲2̲

SWAN OF THE EAST

EDWIN P. HOYT

SWAN OF THE EAST

THE LIFE AND DEATH OF THE
GERMAN CRUISER *EMDEN* IN WORLD WAR I

Abridged from The Last Cruise of the *Emden*

THE   MACMILLAN   COMPANY,   NEW   YORK

For Dinny,
who always did love a good adventure story.

The Macmillan Company, New York
Collier-Macmillan Canada, Ltd., Toronto, Ontario
Library of Congress catalog card number: 68–23067
Printed in the United States of America

FIRST PRINTING

CONTENTS

Maps showing the course of the Emden
appear on pages 32–33 and 140–141.

SWAN OF THE EAST

1. THE SHIP

THEY CALLED her the Gray Swan of the East because of her graceful lines. Wherever Europeans met in Asia this handsome German cruiser was mentioned, for she was one of the most impressive warships ever built, not because she was large or important, but because she was perfectly suited for her job.

Seine Majistäts Schiffe *Emden*, His Majesty's Ship, constructed in Danzig in 1907–1908, was one of those German cruisers envisioned and launched in the warmth of the Imperial high command's hopes for domination of the seven seas.

Before World War I very few of the world's naval leaders had much confidence in the powers of the submarine to wreak damage on warships. Nor was the concept of unrestricted naval warfare of any kind yet invented. War was a relatively leisurely matter, particularly on the high seas. There were rules to govern it, developed in a series of international conferences. It was proper to sink a vessel that belonged to the enemy, of course. This was accomplished

1

by the warship's overtaking the enemy, calling on her to stop, even firing a shot across her bow. The enemy merchantman, having stopped, would then be boarded, and the boarding officer would present his compliments to the captain of the enemy merchant ship, then inform him as to the fate of his vessel. It might be towed into a port belonging to the attacker. Its cargo might be transferred to the warship or to one of her retinue of coalers. (No warship, in these days before the diesel engine, could hope to travel long without coaling.) The enemy merchantman might be sunk. Usually this was accomplished by opening the seacocks of the vessel and allowing her to go down, aided perhaps by a few small explosive charges placed strategically in the bottom. Sometimes, if the attacker was in a hurry or wished to give his crew some gun practice, the merchantman was made into a target. But all this was done after the crew and the passengers had been safely removed from the scene of action. They were not usually abandoned to their fate in lifeboats; the finest traditions of naval warfare called for the protection of the crew and passengers and the guarantee of their safety by the attacker. Consequently, those who wished to practice warfare in the grand tradition used the first ship they might capture in their train of suppliers as what the French called a *chiffonier* and the Germans a *Lumpensammler*. Both words mean junkman in English. The *Lumpensammler* was the ship saved to house prisoners. When it became an overloaded ark, it was dispatched from the train with orders to seek a neutral port and deliver the human cargo safe and sound.

A neutral vessel, under the carefully wrought rules of naval warfare, might be stopped on the high seas and searched. (The Americans in particular objected to this practice very strenuously.) If it was found to be carrying war matériel, it too might be captured. War matériel was to become very broadly defined, and seizures were to be handled most ineptly by the belligerents, contributing to the swift breakdown of the rules of civilized warfare in World War I. But in the *Emden*'s day warfare was a civilized matter, with the fighting to be conducted between men matched as nearly as possible, and with civilians and noncombatants to be protected even at the cost of the lives of the fighters.

Since the submarine did not seriously enter the calculations of the naval leaders in the first decade of the twentieth century, they devised other plans for the harassment of the supply lines of their potential enemies. The raider was considered to be their major weapon for this use. The raider was the successor to the privateer of the days of the American Revolution. Governments could afford to commission and operate their own raiders, so the spoils of war were no longer turned to private profit, but the principle was the same. A raider might be a fast converted merchantman armed with only one or two pieces of naval artillery. Even one gun capable of piercing holes beneath the water line of a merchant ship would make a raider effective against unarmed merchantmen. These converted merchantmen were called auxiliary cruisers. They came in all sizes and varieties. It was enough that they be able to sport some kind of gun to terrorize and if necessary to sink enemy ships.

The Germans led all other nations in the development of a special naval vessel designed for this purpose. This was the small unarmored cruiser. Such was S.M.S. *Emden*. During the course of her building someone in the Berlin government had the idea that it would be useful and binding in a patriotic way to name this series of cruisers after various

German cities. So Emden, a port on the Ems River and once, under the Brandenburgs, a leader in the development of the German maritime industry, was chosen to sponsor this particular little cruiser. The mayor of the city journeyed to Danzig on May 26, 1908, and in the name of the Emperor Wilhelm II he christened the new ship.

The *Emden* displaced 3,650 tons. Her two steam-driven engines, fired by coal, could attain a speed of 24.5 knots. If she was operated at reduced speed and handled carefully, she could travel as far as six thousand miles without recoaling. This, at the time of her launching, was regarded as a major breakthrough in the logistics of naval warfare. She was armed with ten guns of 4.1 inches, which were capable of rapid fire. These were not large for naval guns; a British light cruiser, for example, might mount guns of more than 6 inches in size; but the *Emden* was not built to fight other cruisers. She was built to be the twentieth-century equivalent of the privateer. The French had a word for this class of cruiser: they called it the *corsaire*.

On commissioning, the *Emden* carried a force of seventeen officers and 361 men under a captain who, in the tradition of the German Navy, also commanded one of the two watches that alternated in the routine operation of the vessel. Her trial runs were held between July and September 1909, and she functioned as nearly perfectly as the admiralty had any right to expect. For a time she was kept in home waters. On April 1, 1910, she became officially a part of the Imperial German Navy in a ceremony in which her flag was raised amid streamers and the hoots of the whistles of accompanying vessels. Captain Vollerthun sat down that day and wrote to the authorities of the city of Emden, describing the performance of the ship and her mission in the world, and with due patriotic ceremony the message was received and publicized. And a month later the *Emden* was off around the world to begin her mission: the strengthening of Germany's bonds of empire.

In the fashion of the steel warships of the period, the *Emden* was long, low, and rakish in design. The breakwater of her bow projected farther forward at the water line than at the level of the main deck—a hangover from the days of ramming and the use of ironclads as ships of all work.

Dark round portholes dotted her hull forward and aft. Most of her living and working space was below the main-deck level. The superstructure was dominated by two tall masts which served as radio towers, lookout stations, and signaling posts, by the three towering stacks, and by the bridge superstructure, which stood some three decks high, about halfway up the smokestack level. She sported two torpedo tubes in addition to her other armament, and her turrets, inconspicuous as they might appear in the overall view, made her a formidable weapon to any vessel but a larger cruiser or a battleship.

She was armored, although she was not called an armored cruiser because the steel plating that protected her was relatively light. Her armor deck was only between one and two inches thick. The command tower was more heavily armored, however, since it projected above the ship; here and also at the vulnerable water line the armor was three to four inches thick. Altogether, with her length of 128 yards and width of fifteen yards, she was a slim and graceful ship. In the Far East she was known among German Navy men as the Swan of the East.

In September 1910, the *Emden* arrived in Tsingtao, China, headquarters of the German East Asia Squadron. On

January 5, 1912, Captain von Restorff assumed command of the cruiser.

Von Restorff's tenure lasted just over a year. When the relief of the East Asia Squadron arrived in Tsingtao in May 1913, it brought Korvettenkapitän Karl von Müller from a workroom in the Reichsmarineamt in Berlin to fulfill a personal dream: command of a small cruiser.

2. THE MEN OF THE EMDEN

HE MEN of the *Emden* were distinguished, from the beginning, for their loyalty and sense of responsibility, above all else. They were good, faithful servants of Germany and the Kaiser, and for this quality one man was responsible above all others. He was Karl von Müller, captain of the *Emden.*

Von Müller represented all that was best in the Prussian officer class. That was his background and his tradition; his was an officer family for as far back as anyone could remember. Both his grandfathers were officers in the army. His father was a colonel in the Prussian Army and then in the German Army. On his mother's side the military tradition was strengthened by a political tradition. His mother was born Charlotte Bennigsen. Her brother, Rudolf von Bennigsen, was a leader of the German nationalist movement early in the century.

Von Müller's service was typical of the training of young German officers, first in the cadet corps at Plon, then to Berlin and Lichtenfeld for schooling and the discipline of military life. His first school ship was the *Stosch,* his next was the famous cruiser *Gneisenau,* aboard which he traveled to South America and the United States on training cruises. Even then his most noteworthy characteristic was emerging. Kapitän-zur-See Persius of the *Gneisenau* singled him out for commendation in his reports to Berlin for his orderliness and "painful conscientiousness." On this service von Müller came to know Meyer-Waldeck very well; later they would renew acquaintance when von Müller took the *Emden* and Meyer-Waldeck served as the last governor of Kiaochow Province, which included Tsingtao.

Promotions came regularly for the earnest young officer. In the autumn of 1894 he was promoted to Leutnant-zur-See, three years later to Oberleutnant-zur-See, in 1903 to Kapitänleutnant, in 1908 to Korvettenkapitän, the rank he held when he came to the *Emden.* His experience was broad and his knowledge was extensive by 1913. He had been signal officer on the old ship-of-the-line *Moltke,* officer of the guard on the cruiser *Geflon.* He had served aboard the torpedo school ship *Blucher,* on the flagship *Blitz,* and on the armored coastal cruiser *Agir.* He had been to minesweeping school and torpedo school, and he had served for two years on the light cruiser *Schwalbe* in colonial waters. Most of the time the *Schwalbe* was stationed on the coast of East Africa.

For two years he was adjutant of the First Naval Division, stationed at Kiel. Then in 1902 he became artillery officer on the battleship *Kaiser Wilhelm I.* He had served as a staff officer at sea and at the admiralty. He had served royalty, as aide to Prince Heinrich, grand admiral and commander of the flagship *Deutschland.* Finally, he had sat at the knee of the great Alfred von Tirpitz in the Reichsmarineamt in Berlin, and there he had applied for command of a light cruiser, to receive the *Emden*.

Von Müller had been decorated several times for service and bravery. He held the Red Order of the German Eagle, fourth class with a crown, which signified its second presentation. He held the Imperial Crown Order, third class, with swords to increase its honor.

Von Müller's men, while with one exception not so distinguished as himself, were competent representatives of His Majesty's Imperial Navy. Kapitänleutnant Hellmuth von Mücke, second in command, was the tall blond Saxon who might well be mistaken for a Prussian. He was correct and nearly as disciplined in his manners as von Müller. Kapitänleutnant Ernst Gaede, the gunnery officer, twenty-nine years old, was a Prussian like his captain, the son of a Hanover judge and the graduate of Bromberg's gymnasium and the grammar school at Königsberg before he became a professional member of the naval officer corps.

Kapitänleutnant Gropius, the ship's navigator, was thirty-one years old, a gay young bachelor who was noted for his personal bravery. He had been sabre ensign on the *Weissenberg* in 1904 and during maneuvers had saved the life of a seaman, exposing himself to great danger to do so.

The *Emden* was signally honored by the royal family in 1914, for aboard her was the Kaiser's nephew, Prince Franz Joseph von Hohenzollern, serving as second torpedo officer. The prince was a young bachelor, too, as were most of the officers. He put on no princely airs among his fellows but was as ready to stand his turn at paying for the beer as von Mücke or the others. His companion, assigned to him by the naval authorities, was Leutnant Ernst von Levetzow, a nephew of another of Germany's naval heroes. He was about the same age as the prince, in his late twenties.

One of the favorites with the crew and even with the quiet, stern captain, who played no favorites, was Leutnant Albert Bernhard Maria von Guerard, son of one of Düsseldorf's finest families. His grandfather was one of Germany's best-known eye surgeons, the Professor Doktor Mooren. His father was Theo von Guerard, a career naval officer. He was the jolliest of them all, a slender young man with pleasant manners and a bright eye. Von Müller regarded him as potentially the finest officer aboard his ship. He was the youngest of the group who had the captain's ear; he was only twenty-one years old and would not celebrate his twenty-second birthday until after the war began. Young as he was, Leutnant von Guerard was serving that summer as adjutant of the ship. He was the man responsible for the relations of the *Emden* with the ever correct, ever watchful, ever demanding division commanders of the squadron and the fleet.

Except for a handful of older petty officers and specialists, the enlisted men of the *Emden* were surprisingly young. Most of them were under twenty-one. They were single, boisterous, and good-natured. They were aware of their extreme good fortune in being assigned duty in East Asia rather than in the rough North Sea, where training exercises were conducted summer and winter under the eyes of the high command.

The commander of the German East Asia Squadron was Vice-Admiral the Graf (Count) Maximilian von Spee, a nobleman but an outstanding officer of His Majesty's Navy. The admiral's command was a huge one, speaking geographically.

He was responsible for everything in the Pacific, including the Indian Ocean, as far as the Cape of Good Hope and the Red Sea on one side and the coast of Mexico on the other side, north to the end of the world, and south to the waters of Australia. The squadron of half a dozen cruisers and smaller supporting vessels represented German might in this area. One small cruiser, in recent years, had been detailed semi-annually to serve in Mexican waters, to make trips to South America as diplomacy demanded, and to show the flag where it would help. There had been talk of this year sending the *Emden* to Mexico, but in the end it was decided that the *Nürnberg* would go there, and she had gone at the first of the year. It was time to relieve her. Again the *Emden* was mentioned, but again the admiral made other plans. The light cruiser *Leipzig* was at that moment to be engaged in a state visit in the waters of Japan. The international situation had continued to be so undecided all spring that Admiral Spee was looking to his coal supplies. Japan was a thousand miles closer to Mexico than Tsingtao, and by leaving from Tokyo Bay the *Leipzig* could beg her coal supply from the Japanese. Thus the coal dumps in Tsingtao, replenished at great trouble and expense by ship each month, could be saved so much fuel for whatever needs might come.

In June the cruiser squadron lay at anchor in Tsingtao, and the new men were taught the rules of their ships. Every day was given over to drills and inspections. The ship was burnished down watch on watch, the crews were trained to run out the ten guns, to use the depth charges she carried at the taffrail, to play the hoses for damage control. The stokers were taught how to keep the fires burning brightly without smoking overmuch. The torpedo men were taught to use their weapons. Youngsters were given doses of discipline for thoughtless infractions, and old sailors were reminded that the East Asia Squadron demanded as much spit and polish as did the ships in Germany.

There was practice in gunnery, with the squadron steaming majestically out of harbor into the Yellow Sea, one cruiser towing the targets for another, or a gunboat put to service for the task. The admiral wanted to be sure that his ships were all ready for any action that might develop, and he had very little time in which to make ready. For the next three months the squadron would be scattered, because the *Scharnhorst* and *Gneisenau* were destined to make a journey of state to the South Seas and the *Emden* was to go to Shanghai for a few weeks.

During the training there were embarrassing incidents. One day the admiral came aboard the *Emden* to observe the progress of Captain von Müller's replacements. His launch was drawn alongside and he was piped with proper ceremony aboard the ship, as the deck crew stood at attention in their summer whites and the captain gave the admiral the bridge.

Steam was up and von Müller gave the order for slow ahead and navigated the long silvery ship out of the harbor and into the bay. Half speed was rung down and registered in the engine room, and then full speed. The foamy tops of the waves of open water sped by at more than twenty knots. Then and only then did anyone notice the admiral's launch, bouncing merrily against the side of the *Emden* to which she was so neatly tied, beating a merry tattoo with her lapstrake hull against the armor plating.

The admiral was not amused. Captain von Müller, that disciple of naval perfection, was chagrined and upset by the laxness of his crew in attending to a normal, routine matter. (The admiral's boat crew was not without fault either, but this did not matter, nor was it ever considered as an excuse by von Müller.) A lesser captain might have had someone's head for the error. Von Müller took the blame upon himself, and except for ordering the ship stopped and the launch disengaged and hoisted aboard, he never mentioned the matter to his subordinates. He did not need to shout. Such was the respect in which he was held by all his men that the incident served to strengthen morale aboard the *Emden* and to prove to every doubter what a great captain they had.

A few days after this incident the *Emden* moved out of the main harbor and into the repair harbor, where she went into drydock for repair of damage she had suffered to the propeller of her port screw. This meant only a minimum crew would be needed aboard the *Emden* for a week, so Adjutant von Guerard was kept busy figuring the shore leave coming to the officers and men, furloughs, and extra passes, and arrangements were made for a virtual vacation from duty for most of the crew for the week. The other ships had extra duty that week, for the German Navy was playing host to the British. Vice-Admiral Sir Martyn Jerram, commander of the cruisers in China waters, brought his flagship, the H.M.S. *Minotaur,* for a state visit. This meant a round of balls and dinners and entertainments for the officers and beer halls and football games and rowing contests for the men.

The stay of the *Minotaur* lasted four days. By the time she was sent out of the harbor, band playing a busy march and flags flying, the damage to the *Emden* was repaired and she was fit for sea.

She was ready, then, to perform her duties of hospitality and social responsibility when the *Scharnhorst* and *Gneisenau* set forth on their visit to the South Seas, which would take them away from Tsingtao all during the summer months and might extend deep into autumn.

The men of the *Emden* would train in Tsingtao for the next few weeks, using one of the gunboats to tow targets and simulate attacks. Then, toward the end of July, the *Emden* was to steam to Shanghai, for her own visit of state.

After the departure of the admiral for the south, the officers and men of the *Emden* were able to relax a little. Discipline did not give way, but the absence of the commanding officer of the flotilla removed a certain extra strain that was always present when he was in harbor.

Captain von Müller worried less, for one thing, although the men of his ship would hardly know that, for he seldom saw them except in line of duty, and then he nearly always seemed abstracted. The men loved and respected von Müller for his fairness and his good nature, but there was no close bond of affection between captain and crew. He always seemed to have his nose in a book, a naval book of some kind. He was soft-spoken and quiet. They really did not know him at all, or know that at home he was jolly and much loved by his family. The "painful conscientiousness" had never disappeared from his make-up. He was determined that he would be the best captain of the best light cruiser in German service, and to accomplish this he did not relax for so much as a minute.

On the departure of the *Scharnhorst* and the *Gneisenau,* von Müller gave the days over to gunnery, practicing mine laying and recovery, practice of explosion of mines, and seamanship. Kapitänleutnant von Mücke had two great enthusiasms, and von Müller allowed him to indulge them. Von Mücke felt the men of the German Navy did not normally have enough practice and were thus slow and incompetent in the actual manning of the guns. So the crew of the *Emden* spent an hour or so every day in practice, far more than they were used to on other ships.

Von Mücke's other enthusiasm was swimming. He wanted every man aboard the *Emden* to be able to swim and to swim well. This was not so much because of the possibility of the ship's crew saving itself by swimming en masse from their sinking vessel in time of disaster, but to eliminate accidents and to keep the men physically fit and to increase their endurance. So he went to the captain with his ideas, filled with bright, blond vigor and the zeal of a promoter, and von Müller was amused and indulged him. While other men of the German Navy sat in the afternoons, the men of the *Emden* swam. Von Mücke supervised them, and so did Kapitänleutnant Gaede and Marine Engineer Stoffer, who had been converted in much conversation in the late hours of parties to von Mücke's enthusiastic point of view.

Hellmuth von Mücke had one other quirk, or so his seamen thought at that time. He said the men of the ship must be able to take care of themselves. In Tsingtao, as in so many other ports of the Far East, the actual loading of the ship was done by Chinese coolies. They brought in the coal. They brought in the provisions. They packed and stacked these supplies and the guns and arms and even some of the ammunition. The life of the seaman was easy; except on the high seas his manual labor was concerned with his specialty, as a rule. In port the coolies did the work. Von Mücke did not like this one bit. He kept after the captain to allow him to use the men for the work, and the captain agreed that the slovenly practices of Europeans in the Far East would be changed in the case of the *Emden*. So the first officer won another argument that he felt was peculiarly important, and the men of the *Emden* became proficient at supplying and actually loading their own ship in fast time. Von Mücke had a reason for this beyond the naval officer's love of a tight ship and a ready crew. He was certain that in a very short time the *Emden* was going to need these skills. He was the principal reader of newspapers and magazines and the student of international affairs aboard the *Emden*. He studied politics as well as naval guides. He was certain that Germany was going to war, even perhaps with the men of the British *Minotaur* with whom they had become so friendly a few weeks before, but certainly with the Russians and possibly with the French. He was also sure that the *Emden* was going to war before summer was over that year.

3. THE EMDEN
GOES TO WAR

KAPITÄNLEUTNANT VON MÜCKE was not the only man in Tsingtao to feel that war was coming to the world very soon, although from a glance around the city on any given day it would have been hard to find notable evidence of fears or preparations. Life went on almost as usual. There was polo at the country club and riding for those officers who had the time. There was entertainment at the officers' club ashore and at the Tsingtao Club, and there were the big public restaurants, the Bude and the Dachsal, where officers and civilians met to talk. The talk was the key.

One night, sitting at a table at the Dachsal, officers from the *Emden* got to talking with Captain Julius Lauterbach, commander of the North German Line steamer *Staatssekretär Kraetke*. Lauterbach was a huge bull of a man. He weighed 255 pounds, by his own statement, and he was prone to announce that he had no intention of losing a pound of it, then downing another stein of beer. The men of the *Emden* could not have asked for a better intelligence agent. Lauterbach knew everyone on the China coast and everyone knew him: the big fat jolly German skipper of the mailboat.

On this night Lauterbach asked one of the officers present at the table if he could not begin serving his reserve officer's annual stint of two months immediately. It came out then that Lauterbach was expecting war within the next two months. So on his way south, he had made it a point to stop in for a talk with the senior officers of the East Asia Squadron and apply for his reserve service to begin. It was decided that he would serve on the *Emden,* for the *Emden* was to be left as station ship in Tsingtao while the remainder of the squadron went off about its routine duties.

Lauterbach came back to Tsingtao for duty and boarded the *Emden* on June 15. As an Oberleutnant-zur-See he was to join the other senior lieutenants as a watch officer. He soon had von Mücke even more convinced that war was coming, and the others began to listen to his tales.

Two weeks later came news of the assassination on June 28 of Archduke Franz Ferdinand of Austria-Hungary. This was the incident the big powers of Europe had been welcoming or dreading, depending on their point of view. Europe was divided in two parts. On one side was the ambitious German empire, whose Prussian generals wanted war to increase their territory and power in Europe. The major ally of Germany was the Austro-Hungarian empire of the Hapsburg family. Over many years the Austro-Hungarian empire had expanded until it controlled peoples who were neither Austrian nor Hungarian. Some of these peoples were Slavs, and since the Russians were Slavs, too, they felt a kinship and protective spirit toward the other Slavs. Sarajevo, where the Archduke Franz Ferdinand was killed, was a part of Serbia, a Slavic country. The Austro-Hungarian government decided to punish Serbia, even though it was known that Russia would be angry. The Austro-Hungarians were willing to risk war. The Germans wanted war.

On the other side, the Russians were allied with the French and the British. If Russia went to war with Germany, then France and Britain were bound by treaties to help Russia. Other countries were then bound by various other treaties to go to war on one side or the other. If war came, it would be like a giant landslide, gathering force constantly as it swept along toward the final smash.

At Tsingtao the news of the assassination came to the men of the *Emden* by cable, but that was all they had. It was two weeks before the details were known; all during the crisis the people of the Orient were living two weeks behind events.

In Tsingtao most of the people lived on in the blissful quiet of superior beings who dwelt above and not with the people of the land. It was exciting and interesting to read of events in Berlin and Vienna and Moscow, but there was a relaxed certainty of belief that the crisis would evaporate as so many crises had before.

Aboard the *Emden* only because of von Mücke's fervor was the pace of training increased. Even so, the pace would have been relatively swift, for this was training time. And so Oberleutnant Lauterbach joined the ship and its watches, and Kapitänleutnant Gaede began working the fat off him and the others in intensive exercises in gunnery and seamanship. No one minded. The exercise was offset by long cool evenings of storytelling and laughter.

As tension increased, the training continued.

On July 24, the Austro-Hungarian cruiser *Kaiserin Elizabeth* steamed into Tsingtao. The habits of peacetime were still strong, so the newcomers were greeted by the royal welcome the Imperial Navy could give its friends. There were contests and games again, and the officers took the Austrians on motoring trips to the Lauchan mountains and gave musical dinner parties to amuse them. Those who concerned themselves with basic matters reasoned that the obsolete *Kaiserin Elizabeth* had more than hospitality on her mind when she sought the safety of Tsingtao's landlocked bay. The tension increased.

Now it became known on the *Emden* that Captain von Müller and Adjutant von Guerard were in constant wireless communication with the squadron—and, more important, and most unusual, with Berlin. The *Emden* was, in effect, the listening post for the absent cruiser squadron and its connection with higher authority.

By July 29, when Berlin announced that Austria-Hungary had declared war on Serbia, the tension was almost unbearable. Captain von Müller began mobilizing all the resources of Germany in the China area. This was his duty as senior officer of the station. He called in the gunboats from the Yangtze River and other points along the coast. He ordered the supply steamers for the squadron to load supplies. He ordered the mail steamers to come into port, or, if they could not reach the German colony, to find their way to neutral ports and stay there. This meant to get out of Russian and English waters. The mail steamers would be equipped if possible and sent out as auxiliary cruisers if war came, with the mission of disrupting enemy shipping. The freighters would become part of the supply train of the cruiser squadron.

The next day Captain von Müller called a meeting of all commanders of vessels on the *Emden*. When the vessel commanders arrived they found the *Emden* on a war footing. Early in the morning von Mücke had called the officers together and given them the order: *auspacken,* which meant prepare the ship for action. Only the officers were given this blunt order. Captain von Müller instructed his first officer to tell the crew to make ready for maneuvers, but few of the crew believed the captain really expected to go on training maneuvers.

Later, the captain assembled his officers in his cabin and told them about the political situation. War with Russia was expected at any moment.

The group that assembled in his cabin later that day included the commanders of three gunboats and one torpedo boat. Other gunboats were on their way, one from Shanghai, one from its station up the Yangtze, but it would be several days before they would arrive. One of the gunboats, the *Kormoran,* was badly in need of repairs. It was decided that she would be put into drydock immediately. The coaler *Elsbeth* was to be dispatched with coal to the squadron as soon as she could be loaded. The various gunboats were assigned war duty: either to be at the disposal of the commander of the garrison at Tsingtao or to go off on special duty as escorts for auxiliary cruisers.

Aboard the *Emden,* preparations had been made swiftly to go on a war footing. This meant the officers and men had to unload all their purchases. Civilian clothes went ashore. So did all surplus belongings.

There was no leisure now for long evenings at the officers' club or days spent playing tennis or lolling on the beach. A detail was sent to the post office and another to the telegraph office in Tsingtao to await any messages that might come for the *Emden* or Captain von Müller and to rush them to the ship so they would arrive without delay.

One last shore leave was granted on the night of July 30 so the men and officers could tidy up their affairs. The next day in Berlin the German government sent ultimatums to Russia and to France warning against mobilization. Aboard the *Emden* the tension of the past few days was replaced by frenzied activity. Gunnery Officer Gaede took as many men as von Mücke would allow him to load ammunition from the dump nearby. The captain ordered the removal of all the paneling that the officers had installed in the wardroom and in their quarters. It would be dangerous in case of action, he said, because the wood might splinter and burn. So von Mücke had to assign men to that task. Still others were occupied with exchange and the securing of new torpedoes from the mine depot. At six o'clock they would begin coaling, which meant an all-night job for some of the crew and several of the officers, even though the actual loading was done by Chinese coolies.

That day came a cable from Berlin which announced that a serious state of tension existed between Germany and Austria on the one side and the Triple Entente of Russia, France, and Britain on the other.

The *Elsbeth* moved to the coaling station that day, preparing to leave to supply the cruiser squadron in the south, which was bound to be short of coal, moving so far from home in waters where native coal did not exist. Couriers brought the sacks of mail for the squadron to the *Elsbeth*, and Captain von Müller prepared dispatches and papers that would be sent to the admiral aboard this ship.

There were a hundred details to be managed in a few

hours. Transport had to be sent to the Tsingtao Naval Hospital to bring back the crewmen of the *Emden* who were suffering only from minor illness and could be expected to return to duty shortly. Kapitänleutnant Gaede was dispatched to make a round of the German shipping companies in the city and warn them to wireless all their merchant ships and tell them to seek neutral ports at once.

Steam was raised in the boilers of the *Emden* and live ammunition was brought forward for the guns. The torpedoes were fitted with warheads and the dummy practice heads were sent ashore.

All this activity was leading to a point. By evening the point was reached. Captain von Müller ordered the ship to prepare to leave port. In his indefatigable reading of naval history and tactics he had come across the story of the Russian warships *Warjag* and *Korejetz* during the Russo-Japanese War of 1905. They had been in harbor at Chemulpo (now Inchon, Korea) when the war began and had remained so long inside that they were blockaded by the Japanese before they could escape and were trapped like rats. Von Müller did not intend to be trapped in the landlocked harbor of Tsingtao by an English or French warship. He intended to get outside and fight if war was declared.

At seven o'clock that night the order was given and the *Emden* began to move out of the coaling dock and then into Kiaochow Bay. The *Elsbeth* tagged behind her.

As the ship steamed toward the bay entrance the crew were informed that they would go on a war-watch basis. In peacetime the watches were split into four parts, and a man stood watch only six hours in twenty-four when at sea. But with the war watch the ship was divided into two watches, one commanded by the captain and the other by the first officer, and it was four hours on and four hours off, with the men of the watch always at battle stations.

Outside the harbor the drum and bugle suddenly blared with the call to clear the ship for action. The surprised officers and crew rushed to comply. When an hour passed they relaxed. The men continued to stand at their guns, at the searchlights, in the torpedo room, on the command bridge, and in the high lookout towers on the masts, but they saw nothing and heard nothing. It grew oppressively hot within the ship; the portholes were closed to extinguish all lights, and the blower system was shut down. It was particularly hot below decks, where the ship's hospital was located. Some relief came when the *Emden* ran into a storm and the captain ordered the portholes opened in the cover of the rain and clouds. Still the blowers remained off until the alert was ended and normal duty stations were in order.

The *Emden* set her course southeast, toward the Pacific Islands where the squadron lay, and steamed in that direction until eleven o'clock that night. She was providing escort and company for the *Elsbeth,* hoping to set her on her way to safety. At eleven, or 2300 hours, the *Emden* turned away, wishing the *Elsbeth* godspeed. Captain von Müller laid the course for Quelpart (now Chejus) Island, just off the normal steamer lanes. He intended to stay out on cruise until the political situation in Europe was resolved. Every few minutes messages were flashed back and forth between the ship and the wireless station atop the hill back in Tsingtao, but the crisis was not resolved on this night of July 31. The next day, August 1, the *Emden* lurked on the edge of the steamer routes, keeping sharp lookout, but not ready yet to attack any vessel she might see. The lookout under these conditions was all in the hands of officers. They climbed the masts and took charge of the stations. Other officers and men stood at every high point on the ship, their eyes trained on the horizon, looking for telltale smoke or sail. But on August 1, while the wireless buzzed with messages, none were conclusive, and in the calm glassy sea there was nothing to see, not even one of the tiny fishing junks that usually sailed so far out to sea in good weather.

Everyone aboard the *Emden* was growing edgy. The tension of the previous days in Tsingtao was as nothing compared to this, which could mean life or death to the ship and its crew, for if the *Emden* did not get the news, and war was declared, and she was sighted by a belligerent she did not see, her end might come at any time. She must know if Germany was at war and with whom Germany was at war. The radiomen of the *Emden* faithfully carried each message to the captain as it was received, but this was not enough. First Officer von Mücke took to dropping into the radio shack and waiting as the messages were coming in. At about three o'clock in the afternoon he came in again.

"Any strange traffic?" he asked, and he picked up the receiver himself. From the receiver came a loud crackling, and the first officer jerked the instrument from his ear. The English dogs were so close that their radioing nearly broke his eardrums, he said, and reminding the radio men to report anything immediately to the bridge he strode off to inform the captain.

Late that afternoon the wireless crackled and the operators became excited. One of them rushed to the captain on the bridge to deliver the message that Berlin had ordered the mobilization of the army and the fleet. Physically, this meant very little to the men of the *Emden,* who were as completely mobilized as the men of a warship can be, but some realized that now war was certain.

At just past two in the afternoon the next day Captain von Müller appeared on the poop, holding a message slip in his hand. Germany was at war with Russia. War with France and England seemed inevitable, he said. Like Germany, the *Emden* had not sought war, he said, but now he was going to head the ship in the direction of Vladivostok, for here his intelligence reports told him was the greatest concentration of Russian and French naval vessels in the Pacific region. Here they might expect to meet the enemy. "Our first duty," he said, "is to raid the commerce of the enemy."

Of the major French and Russian warships the only one the *Emden* might really wish to meet was the *Yemtschuk,* the Russian light cruiser stationed in Vladivostok. She was a fair match for the *Emden.* The Russian heavy cruiser *Askold* could blow the *Emden* out of the water quickly enough, and so could the French heavy cruisers *Montcalm* and *Dupleix,* which were known to be somewhere in Asian waters—probably in Vladivostok. Von Müller would fight another warship if he had to, but his orders were to avoid a fight and concentrate on enemy shipping. He did not say so much to his crew. Since the Russians and French were in the area, he said, "It is therefore probable that we shall encounter them. In that event, I feel confident that I can rely upon my men."

It was a low-keyed statement, typical of the man. It brought three lusty cheers from the crew for the Kaiser.

Von Müller now conferred with Oberleutnant Lauterbach, who, a steamer captain in civil life, was an expert on the movement of steamer traffic in the region. Lauterbach suggested that they move into the Tsushima Straits between

Japan and Korea, to intercept Russian ships bound between Vladivostok and Shanghai. This move brought a certain amount of danger, because the *Emden* still did not know what part the Japanese intended to play in this war. They suspected that the Japanese intended to attack Tsingtao, but they did not know for sure, and they could not act against the Japanese until war came.

The other great unknown was England. But by moving northward von Müller decreased his chances of running into any English vessels.

At a steady cruising speed of fifteen knots the *Emden* moved north and east, through the straits, and then due north. The night was moonless and black. The *Emden* ran dark, her smoke control in effect, and the only sign of her presence was the throbbing of the engines and the churning of the phosphorescent water of her bow wave and her wake.

At midnight the captain lay down for a little sleep and the port war watch took over. First Officer von Mücke made his first tour of inspection, then settled down on the bridge in the blackness to peer into the night.

Nothing.

At four o'clock the captain was awakened and took his post on the bridge, while von Mücke went below to his cabin. He had just gotten to sleep when the alarm bells began to shrill. It was a false alarm, only a cloud, which they could not attack. Later they heard strange wireless conversations. It might have been a warship of some kind, but they did not move close enough to find out.

The weather turned rough and the sea began to run high. Von Müller decided to head south again, hoping to find good weather. It was difficult enough to take a green crew into action, to capture and board a merchantman, without trying in heavy seas. On August 3, the *Emden* moved into the west channel of the straits, off the Korean coast. At about two o'clock on the morning of August 4, during a squall, the lookouts spotted the stern light of a vessel. Then the weather closed in and no more could be seen. Four hours later the lookouts saw the masts and stern of a ship ahead. At the same time the other ship spotted the *Emden* and turned away, beginning to make a dense cloud of smoke. The captain ordered more speed and began the chase.

"Action stations!" was the order.

"Oberleutnant Lauterbach to the bridge."

As the steamer came in view Lauterbach took the glass. She had two golden funnels. As she turned it became apparent that she was heading inland toward Tsushima Island. If she could reach the three-mile limit she would be in Japanese territorial waters and immune from attack, protected by the laws of war concerning neutral regions.

Lauterbach recognized her immediately. He had visited on her bridge a dozen times. She was the Russian mail steamer *Rjasan,* an almost new ship of 3,500 tons, equipped with wireless. She was very fast. At nineteen knots the *Emden* was drawing near, but the *Rjasan* was coming closer to safety. The *Emden* might not overhaul her in time.

Von Müller ordered a shot to be fired across the *Rjasan*'s bows. One of the 4.1-inch guns sent a shell well ahead of her. The *Rjasan* disregarded it. The signal "stop at once" was run up the foremast, but this brought no more response. Von Müller ordered Lieutenant Gaede to begin firing across her bow, bringing each shell closer than the one before. Several rounds were fired before one came so close that the Russian captain turned and stopped his ship. Twelve shots had been fired at her.

Von Müller assigned Oberleutnant Lauterbach to lead a boarding crew to take the prize, and Lauterbach ordered his men into a boat. Then, von Mücke reported that the Russian was trying to send out an S.O.S. by wireless. The signal "do not radio" was run up the *Emden's* foremast. It made no difference. The *Emden's* cutter was over the side with Lauterbach and twenty-two men, twenty of them armed and ready for action. The small boat sped across the choppy water to the Russian, now about 150 yards away. The Russians dropped a rope ladder, but on going alongside in the rough sea the cutter was nearly stove against the steel plates of the steamer, the ladder flapping free above. Von Müller considered the situation so dangerous that he dispatched another boat to the rescue of his cutter, but as the boat went over the side, the men on the *Emden* saw the burly Lauterbach grasp the swinging ladder and pull himself up hand over hand, moving wildly back and forth in the air, an involuntary trapeze artist. Even stopped, von Müller could scarcely see 150 yards through the glass, the weather was so foul. Earlier Gaede's firing had been much hampered by the rolling and bucking of the ship, and no one knew which shot had persuaded the Russian to stop.

Lauterbach helped his men board, and then first of all the armed crew took possession of the wireless station. The frantic tapping of the operator suddenly stopped, and aboard the *Emden* nothing more could be heard.

Lauterbach left Wireless Operator Wille in charge of the station, then joined Captain Austin on the bridge.

"I am awfully sorry, captain," he said in German, "but it is my duty to make your ship a prize of war."

"I don't know what you're saying," Captain Austin replied in English. "I do not speak German."

"Well," said Lauterbach, shrugging his big shoulders, "you have forgotten a lot. You knew German well enough a fortnight ago when we were drinking beer together in the club at Tsingtao."

Austin laughed. It was impossible even for an enemy to dislike Lauterbach.

Lauterbach took the ship's papers and after a few minutes of conversation went to the wireless station to report back to the *Emden*. The *Rjasan* was carrying the Russian mail and a very little cargo. But she had some eighty passengers aboard. What was to be done with her?

Von Müller thought about it for a little bit. The cargo was of little value. The passengers could be put into lifeboats and the ship sunk, but the sea was very rough, and the lifeboats might not survive. Further, the *Rjasan* was new and big and nearly as fast as the *Emden*. She would make a good raider. The guns from the ailing gunboat *Kormoran* could be put aboard her and she could be converted into an auxiliary cruiser.

That is what he decided to do with the Russian ship, and he ordered Lauterbach to remain aboard with twelve men and keep control. They would steam into Tsingtao.

Until the two ships came near Tsingtao, the *Rjasan* preceded and the watchful *Emden* followed. But as they neared the port, von Müller took no chances. There just might be enemy warships about, and in case of action, Lauterbach must be given a chance to run for it and make the safety of the harbor while he fought the enemy. He changed the order, and Lauterbach in his prize followed the *Emden* by 1,200 yards.

At dawn the *Emden* reached the entrance to the mine field and the harbor and joined the *C. S. Leiss,* which was waiting for the escort patrol to come out and bring it safely through the newly laid mines. Tsingtao, which could always be seen from the lip of the harbor, was totally dark. Not a light gleamed in the streets.

The *Emden* was expected, for she had been in wireless contact with the shore station for several hours, and near the island of Matau she blinked a signal, which was answered immediately by the entry gun, shot off to warn of the coming ship to the patrol vessels. She was greeted by the gunboat *Jaguar* in a few moments, and the captain and a pilot came aboard to bring the cruiser safely through the mine field. The *Emden* entered harbor at six o'clock in the morning, and the crew could sigh with relief.

Poor Lauterbach, aboard the *Rjasan,* had to sit unprotected outside the mine field for several more hours. At breakfast he was told that he must appear in government court that morning to settle the question of the *Rjasan*'s status as a prize. He escaped the court at lunchtime and appeared at the Tsingtao club, and there he was greeted by what seemed to be all his old friends of the merchant trade.

"Good day, Lauterbach," said one old acquaintance, a merchant captain now in the uniform of a sergeant major. "How was it outside?"

Lauterbach, the genial clown of the China Seas, looked him up and down.

"You should say 'Herr Oberleutnant' when you speak to me," he said. "It's a good thing that you come under military discipline now, young man, very good for you. High time. Stand up, if you please, when you are talking to your superior officer."

For Lauterbach, now one of the men of the *Emden,* had already been to war.

Course of S.M.S. EMDEN, 1914

Scale of Statute Miles

0 200 400 600 800 1,000

Outward sweep — — —
Reverse leg ------
Coaling operations △

N

W   E

S

BRITISH INDIA

ARABIAN SEA

20° N

BOMBAY

CALCUTTA

PURI

BURMA

RANGOON

SI

MADRAS

10° N

PONDICHERRY

COCHIN

KARIKAL

CEYLON

COLOMBO

BAY OF BENGAL

Andaman Is.

Nicobar Is.

Maldive Is.

0°

KHOTA RAJA

SIMALUR

SUMAT

PE

EQUATOR

INDIAN OCEAN

CHAGOS ARCH.

Diego Garcia

80° E

10° S

DESTROYED BY SYDNEY

COCOS KEELING IS.

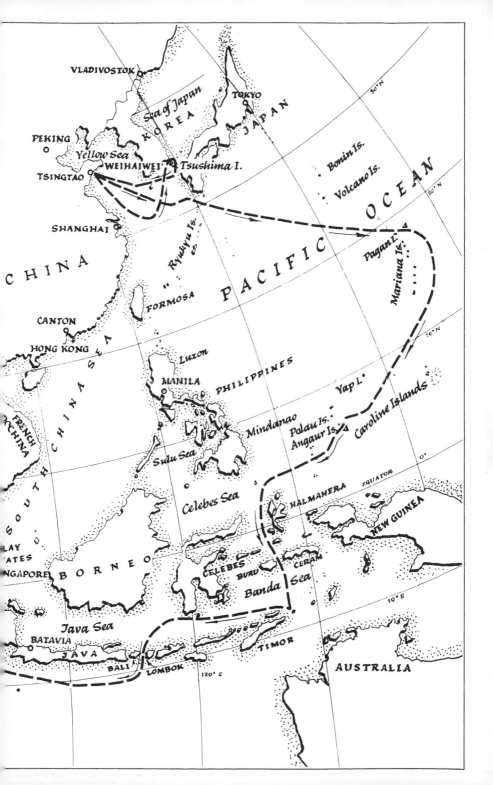

4. TO THE
SOUTH SEAS

CAPTAIN VON MÜLLER secured his ship and left von Mücke in charge of the loading of munitions and the coaling. They were to take on every shell and every ounce of coal they could carry, for no one knew when they would have another chance to supply themselves. Von Mücke put part of his crew to coaling, following his conviction that they must learn to do it quickly because in the future they would be doing it alone.

Von Müller went to the governor's palace after lunch to inform His Excellency of the orders he had received while on the high seas: He would report immediately to the Marianas Islands, where Admiral von Spee lay in harbor awaiting the *Emden* and the *Nürnberg*.

So the entire day of August 6 was spent in furious preparations for the long journey to the harbor at Pagan in the Marianas. The *Emden*'s boats were all put over the side, and crews scurried about the harbor begging and bartering for the luxuries they wanted to carry with them. There was no time to draw from stores any more than the necessities, and no one knew when Tsingtao would receive more soap, cigarettes, and liquor for its own use.

A number of German merchantmen had come into harbor to place themselves at the disposal of their country now that war had begun. Some would be sent out, after guns were put on their decks, to raid enemy shipping. Two were selected to follow the *Emden* south. Captain von Müller went aboard the 9,000-ton passenger ship *Prinz Eitel Friedrich* and told her captain to be ready to sail with him. The *Eitel Friedrich* was just installing the deck guns. She would become a raider. Von Müller also informed the captain of the coaler *Markomannia* that he was to become the supplier and shadow of the *Emden*.

On August 7 the *Emden* embarked more men; added to those she had taken on before sailing to the Tsushima Straits, she now had three new officers, one new deck officer, seventeen new seamen, and thirteen new technicians. A Catholic chaplain came aboard now that the ship was definitely heading for war and gave the sacraments to the Catholics aboard, plus a general absolution.

Von Müller was engaged again in meetings all day long. Dozens of officers from land and other ships came aboard to pay what might be their last respects to the *Emden* and her men. Captain Fahss of the *Markomannia* came aboard for discussions, and so did Korvettenkapitän Thierichens, commander of the *Prinz Eitel Friedrich,* which would accompany the cruiser southward.

Around five-thirty an exhausted First Officer von Mücke could report that the coaling was complete—the *Emden* had taken on an additional 950 tons—and that all supplies which could be obtained had come aboard and were stowed. The ship was ready to sail.

All that day, as the *Emden* coaled, the crews of the *Markomannia* and the *Prinz Eitel Friedrich* had been hard at work to resolve problems of their own. The *Markomannia* completed her coaling and the crew gave her the markings of an English Blue Funnel liner, just to increase her chances of going unrecognized in waters that were certain to be scoured by British ships. The job of concealing the identity of the *Prinz Eitel Friedrich* was more difficult but also more important, since she was to be a fighting ship. The crew spent the entire day repainting the ship.

The Catholic mass was just finished when von Mücke made his report to the captain. One last quick trip ashore to pay a final duty call on the governor at the palace, and Captain von Müller was as ready as he ever would be to leave Tsingtao. He called von Mücke in to give orders, and shortly before 6 P.M. the Swan of the East was ready for her departure, fully laden with the goods of war and steam up.

At six o'clock Captain von Müller walked out onto the bridge deck and gave a signal. A boatswain piped the maneuvering whistle and the members of the deck crew moved to their stations. The ship's band moved to the poop deck and stood in formation. The engines began to tremble a little and the screws of the *Emden* began to turn.

Captain von Müller signaled to cast off. The hawsers from the quay slapped as they hit the water. The wireless began to clatter—already they were receiving signals from the Tsingtao wireless station. The telegraph from bridge to engine room squeaked a little as the signal for more speed was rung down. Obviously in the grip of strong emotion, the commander made a short speech to those staring from the shore, which nearly no one heard above the gathering noises of departure. He was cut off by the beginning of three cheers from the crew of the *Kaiserin Elizabeth,* cheers joined by the hundreds standing on the pier to see their warship go.

"Eyes to starboard," came the shout above the last of the cheers, and turning, the crew could see his excellency the governor, resplendent in his formal naval uniform with medals, passing by in his motor launch, accompanied by his staff. He waved goodbye and his staff all raised their hats. Then they were gone, moving on to pay final respects to the *Prinz Eitel Friedrich.*

Outside the harbor the convoy anchored, and Captain von Müller took the ship's cutter over to the *Markomannia* for a conference to establish their steaming procedure on the route south. Very early in the morning, as the sun was rising, the convoy steamed out through the outer roads and into the steamship lane between Yokohama and Shanghai. Captain von Müller was not wasting any time. If there were prizes to be taken he would take them on his way south to join the squadron.

When the ships left the inner harbor the torpedo boat *S-90* preceded them. She went out to Cape Yunnuisan to see if enemy warships were lurking outside the harbor in wait for the convoy. But there was no blockade, and at the cape the end of the piloted journey came. The pilot descended into his boat, last farewells rang out across the water, and the ships set out, each in her separate direction, alone. The *Prinz Eitel Friedrich* was to adopt one course and steam alone. The *Markomannia* would go ahead, and the *Emden* would join her at the Ryukyu Islands. This left the *Emden* free to maneuver and take prizes if she could.

The *S-90* accompanied them from Yunnuisan as far as Cape Yatau, and then the *Emden* was alone.

For several days she made her way slowly southward,

through the China Sea, traveling toward the rendezvous but also looking out for enemy vessels. Several times she hopefully gave chase to wisps of smoke that appeared on the horizon, but in each case the ship turned out to be a German or a neutral. Several were Japanese, and as far as the *Emden* knew the Japanese were neutrals. They had not yet attacked Tsingtao.

On August 8 the wireless operators picked up messages that told of German victories on land and sea in Europe, and the crew cheered. That evening they intercepted a message for the English ships at sea which rang the alarm: The *Emden* was at sea, said the message, accompanied by two captured merchantmen. Captain von Müller chuckled. He knew whom he had to thank for that message. On the night of their departure they had been trailed through the mine field by a small Japanese steamer.

August 9 was Sunday. The *Emden* had made contact with the *Markomannia* at the Ryukyus.

This was the day the wardroom was torn apart. The curtains had to go. So did the overstuffed furniture and the paneling. The temporary wall between the wardroom and the after battery was torn out, and the carpets were lifted. Every last bit of it went into the furnaces, to speed the *Emden* on and eliminate a fire hazard. Then the wardroom's bare walls were covered with a green paint that the officers could describe only as "poisonous." There was some relief. Prince Franz Joseph was a caricaturist of sorts, and he amused his fellow officers by drawing their pictures on the walls as they were deciding what color to paint the mess. These, too, were covered in the end by the green paint.

On August 12, the *Emden* made her landfall in the

Marianas. The crew had not been told before where they were going; Captain von Müller had kept this information to himself and a handful of trusted officers. Around noon she approached Pagan, whose volcano crown was so distinctive a geographic feature that many of the men knew the island by sight. The *Emden* skirted the island's coast, seeking the harbor, until a ship detached itself from the horizon and steamed forward to investigate this intruder. It was the *Titania,* the squadron's repair and supply ship. She was flying the commandant flag, too, which meant that a ranking naval officer was aboard and the incomer was to obey his instructions. Admiral von Spee had sent the *Titania* out to greet the *Emden* and show her the way to the squadron. A little later, turning into the bay of Pagan, the *Emden* came upon the *Scharnhorst,* the *Gneisenau,* and the *Nürnberg,* all at anchor, surrounded by merchant ships.

As the *Emden* came into the harbor a volley of cheers came from the throats of the men of the cruiser squadron aboard the other ships. A few days before they had heard the radio broadcast the news that the *Emden* had been sunk by the Russian heavy cruiser *Askold.* The admiral and his staff knew this was not true, but they had not enlightened the crews of the squadron ships, so the actual sight of the *Emden* was the first good news the men had had.

The *Emden* threaded her way slowly past the other ships and found an anchorage between the rocky shore and the *Scharnhorst.* She had every right to come to rest beside the flagship. After all, the *Emden* was the first ship of His Majesty's Navy in the Far East to go into battle with an enemy, even a merchant enemy, and very nearly the first German ship anywhere to do so.

5. INTO ACTION

THE *Emden* had scarcely stopped on this warm, sunny day when Fregattenkapitän Karl von Müller was on his way to the *Scharnhorst* to report to his admiral on the activities of the *Emden* and the situation at Tsingtao. The other warships were already taking on coal, which meant to the men of the *Emden* that it would not be a long stay and that the squadron would soon be in action.

Von Müller made his report and returned. The *Emden* would coal the next day, he told his first officer. There would be a meeting of all commanders on the *Scharnhorst* in the morning, and there the strategy of the squadron would be decided and announced.

A barge from the *Gneisenau* came alongside the *Emden* that afternoon to inquire about mail. Thus it was learned that the *Elsbeth* had been sunk or captured, for she had been dispatched from Tsingtao so long before that only a disaster could have prevented her arrival before August 12. She had carried all the mail as well as coal for the squadron. The men of the fighting ships, then, were not to hear from the homeland again.

The work of the next day began at six o'clock in the morning. The ship's bell called the entire crew to duty, and war watches were maintained on a minimal basis for the men so most of them could help with the coaling. Tea and bread was the breakfast for the crew, and then the work began. It would have to be carried out in the morning and evening hours. Midday in the tropics was far too hot for confined work. Fenders were hung over the sides of the *Emden,* the boat davits were made clear all around the ship, and the coaling gangways were laid out. Shovels and empty sacks for coaling were broken out. The awnings on the poop deck were folded up and put away to save them from the soot.

Oberleutnant Lauterbach had been delighted on entering port to see his old command—the *Staatssekretär Kraetke* was one of the bevy of merchant ships at anchor there. Now he took a small boat over to the steamer and personally conned her back to the port side of the *Emden.* There was much shouting and laughter as he brought the big ship smoothly alongside. On the starboard side the *Gouverneur Jaschke* was brought up. Then the dirty work began. The men picked up their shovels and sacks and went into the holds of the merchant ships. The newly promoted Leutnant von Hohenzollern, Prince Franz Joseph, supervised the coaling from the *Staatssekretär Kraetke,* and another of the new lieutenants did the same on the other ship.

While the men made the ship ready for war again, Captain von Müller was engaged in weighty deliberations of policy with the other commanders of the squadron. Around the scuttlebutt it was said that von Müller intended to propose that the *Emden* be detached from the squadron and be allowed to cruise alone in the Indian Ocean. The officers and men of the *Emden* backed this proposal heartily. Almost to a man they were fervent patriots, and they saw England as their primary enemy.

By the morning of August 13 the men of the *Emden* had begun to believe that the *Markomannia* had either been captured or sunk, because she was two full days overdue. But that morning as they choked in the coal dust, the *Markomannia* steamed into the harbor, bearing her five thousand tons of coal, more valuable to the *Emden* than gold or food.

While Captain von Müller was aboard the *Scharnhorst* attending the fateful squadron commanders' meeting, the boats of the *Emden* were sent out by von Mücke to do a bit of trading and scrounging. The important matters were beer and tobacco. The *Emden* had left Tsingtao without adequate supplies of either, since the Tsingtao garrison could spare so little.

Then for the men it was back to work. From the *Scharnhorst* Captain von Müller sent the word that the *Emden*'s coaling must be finished and she must be ready to steam out of the harbor with the squadron by nightfall. In midafternoon it became apparent to First Officer von Mücke that the deadline could not be met without assistance. When he communicated this to his captain, forty men from the *Scharnhorst* were sent to the *Emden* to help with the work.

For the officers, there were some changes. Kapitän-leutnant Metzenthin was detached from the *Emden* and assigned to the *Gneisenau,* where there was a job for one of his senior rank. Two lieutenants came aboard, Roderick Schmidt and S. S. Gyssling. This brought the total personnel aboard the *Emden* to 399.

For the squadron the meeting aboard the *Scharnhorst* was decisive and fateful. Von Müller and the other captains were piped aboard in the morning and went to the admiral's suite, where he was seated in the middle of one side of a long conference table, his staff clustered around him. The squadron commanders sat across from the admiral. All were dressed in their formal summer white uniforms with gold braid and dark trim. The admiral looked peculiarly small and frail and sleepless.

Admiral von Spee gave his opinion of the situation first, punching his finger at the world map on the table in front of him as he spoke. The admiral had decided to take the squadron to the West Coast of the Americas, where it would be possible to assure a supply of coal.

Fregattenkapitän Karl von Müller waited until the senior captains had their say. Then he spoke up.

He was opposed to the move east, he said. According to the plan it would take several months for the ships to cross the Pacific. During that time the fleet would be ineffective against the enemy, except for the energy that might be spent in the search for its whereabouts. If the fleet was located then it could be written off until it moved out again from the West Coast of America. Nor was there enough trade on the route east to make the plan worthwhile.

Von Müller spoke of the future of German sea power and the "fleet in being," a theory which held that the fleet, its whereabouts and strength known, served to immobilize enemy warships without actually engaging in battle. He believed the squadron ought to remain in Asia, but if the problems of coal supply were too difficult, he had an audacious proposal: Why not send one of the light cruisers into the Indian Ocean?

The meeting broke up with the admiral's promise to take von Müller's request under consideration.

Von Müller returned to the *Emden*. The squadron was to be ready to set to sea by five-thirty that afternoon, and it was nearly that when the conference broke up, and the decisions were made. Von Müller returned to his ship at just about the same time that a load of coconuts came in from a shore party. They were broken open by the thirsty coalers. A few moments later a boat came alongside bearing a message for the captain from the admiral. His request was granted. He would break away from the squadron at an appointed signal and the *Emden* would become an independent naval unit.

At five-thirty all ships weighed anchor and formed into two lines. The warships formed to port, the *Scharnhorst* leading the cruisers, the *Emden* tailing them. On the starboard was the line of merchant ships and auxiliary cruisers, headed by the *Prinz Eitel Friedrich*. During the night the starboard line disintegrated, and when dawn broke the warships broke formation disgustedly and went back to round up the stragglers. By eight o'clock it was done, and the squadron was steering a course almost due east. Then came the signal: *"Emden* detached. Good luck."

The *Emden* turned out of line, and from the line of merchantmen the *Markomannia* turned out too, for she was to be the *Emden*'s companion and coaler on this lonely journey into the huge reaches of the Indian Ocean, where the German seaman would have no friends and a thousand enemies would lie in wait for them.

The course was south-southwest. The speed was twelve knots. Even the lowly seamen aboard the *Emden* had the idea that the *Emden* was going off to do battle alone.

6. THE FIRST COALING

OR A DAY and a half the *Emden* steamed along the eastern side of the Marianas until it ran out of that group of islands. The next landfall was Yap, a German possession where there was a wireless station. Captain von Müller ordered his radiomen to make contact with Yap, and they called repeatedly for many hours, but there was no answer. Course was then set for Angaur Island in the Palaus group in the central Pacific Ocean.

The *Emden* steamed steadily at the economical cruising speed of twelve knots, the *Markomannia* following through the clear seas in her wake. The *Markomannia* could make sixteen knots when necessary and for that reason was much prized by the men of the *Emden*.

The voyage to Angaur lasted six days, and then after a brief stopover in the Palaus Islands, the *Emden* again headed out to sea, bound for waters where she hoped to find enemy ships and sink them.

The course of the *Emden* now lay toward a point in the Moluccas. She would steam by Mindanao and right through the Dutch East Indies, then make a right turn and head into the Indian Ocean.

On August 22, the *Emden* crossed the equator. If it had been peacetime there would have been ceremonies of initiation of "pollywogs" to become "old salts," but this was war and there was no time for foolery. The ceremonies were passed over. The next day Captain von Müller was subjected to the worst frustration imaginable: A Japanese passenger ship appeared and although the captain knew that Germany would soon be at war with Japan he had no knowledge whether or not war had really come, and so he would not shoot at what he knew to be an enemy.

They steered between Celebes and Halmahera Islands, but avoided both, trying to keep attention away from the cruiser.

Past the equator they headed through the Moluccan Straits and for Timor. Up came the Nusa-berei Straits, which lie between the northeast shore of Timor and the island of Letti. The *Emden* steamed ahead day and night, blacked out at night, keeping the smoke trail down to avoid detection.

Now the coal on deck had been burned and the bunkers were only half filled, so no matter what would happen the *Emden* must coal again.

On the gray foggy morning of August 25 the *Emden* and the *Markomannia* steamed into a deserted little harbor. The *Emden* took 470 tons from the *Markomannia*. The men were tired and dispirited. War, rather than bringing excitement and glory, was bringing them only heat, bad food, and the never ending filth of coaling. That day Prince Franz Joseph and three of the other lieutenants put down their tunics, picked up sacks of coal, and helped with the physical labor.

The prince offered the men of his port watch cigars if they carried more coal than the men of the starboard watch. So, buoyed by the spirits of their officers, the men made it through quickly, with even a rise to their sagging morale.

On the morning of August 27, the *Emden* approached the Celebes Islands, having steamed for two days down the coast of Timor, along its rocky shore, where the mountains rose from the water to a height of eight thousand feet. At Tanah Jampeia, they steered around the island to enter the bay from the south. Inside, they hoped, they would find a German merchantman waiting.

Instead they found a warship, larger than their own, approaching at full speed with her flags flying. From the distance they could not tell her nationality or her intention. The crew was ready, anxious, eager for action. No time was lost.

"Clear the ship for battle!" rang the cry and the alarm bells clanged and the fifes sounded angrily through the ship.

The men, at action stations, could not see what was happening, but a mile and a half now separated the *Emden* from the larger ship. At 2,500 yards firing could begin easily enough. Captain von Müller held his fire, straining at his glass. Finally when the tension had become nearly unbearable on the bridge he made out her ensign: Dutch. The battle flags were run down from the *Emden*'s foremast and the crew was told to relax. Von Müller had rung up full speed; he now rang the engine down to half, and the two ships closed slowly. The loaders took their asbestos battle gloves off—no danger now that the cartridge cases would burn their hands. The gunners relaxed. The men in the crow's-nests had time to watch the spray scudding up from beneath the Dutchman's bow. The officers on the bridge could note the massive clouds of smoke she made, indicating to them, in their superiority, poor fuel management, or poor fuel.

Still, the quiet that precedes battle held on the decks of the *Emden*. Captain von Müller and Gunnery Officer Gaede stood still, tense even yet, as they would remain until they had passed the warship or the two had stopped for talk.

The ships approached one another slowly, warily. The men on the *Emden* saw that the other ship was the Dutch battleship *Tromp*. But had Holland entered the war against Germany? No one aboard the *Emden* was quite sure. The batteries were told to hold their fire, but the guns continued to be trained on the enemy ship and would be until her intentions were known.

The *Tromp* showed her intentions. Her guns were pointed straight over her bows in a peaceful gesture. So the amenities began.

The bugler was summoned to the deck of the *Emden* and blew attention, which brought the deck crew out to the rails, standing stiffly to honor the other ship. There was no recourse for the *Emden* in courtesy but to enter the bay and anchor, and she did so, the *Tromp* turning in courtesy and following her in.

At anchor, the *Tromp* sent a launch to the *Emden*, showing courtesy, but not so much that her captain bowed before the inferior vessel and came aboard. Then, of course it was necessary for von Müller to return the visit and meet the captain of the other warship, so the steam pinnace was lowered and he went aboard the *Tromp*.

Aboard the Dutch ship, Captain von Müller received bad news. His coaler had arrived off the island, but had been driven away by the *Tromp*.

No warring ships could be permitted to coal in Dutch waters if strict neutrality was to be maintained. Further, warships of the warring nations would be allowed to enter in Dutch waters only once each three months and could then remain only for twenty-four hours. This meant, of course, that there was no chance of the *Emden* playing hit-and-run in the Indian Ocean, then using the Dutch East Indies as a base. One course of action which Captain von Müller had considered was outlawed for him then and there.

The courtesies ended, Captain von Müller returned to the *Emden* with the sad news for his officers. There was no time to consider the problem further, however, because the Dutchman must be fooled. Within an hour the *Emden* and the *Markomannia* steamed out of the harbor and headed northeast, back almost the way they had come, indicating that they were setting out into the Pacific. The *Tromp* accompanied them to the three-mile limit, then dipped her ensign in salute and turned back to her station. The *Emden* steamed on until the *Tromp*'s masthead disappeared over the horizon. Captain von Müller laid the new course, first southeast to draw even farther away from the Dutch battleship, and then due west to make up for lost time. Two days' steaming and the ship would be at the entrance to her dangerous hunting ground, the Indian Ocean. The point of departure was ahead; they would first pass beautiful Bali, and then they would be in the straits, and on the other side were shark-infested waters. In the case of the *Emden,* the sharks were British warships.

7. THE BREAK-THROUGH

IN THE SUMMER of 1914 the Indian Ocean was a British lake. It was surrounded by British possessions or lands where Britain held enough influence to have its way. India and Burma lay on the north. On the west lay the Arabian Peninsula and Africa. South and west was Australia. The only reasonable sea entrance not controlled by the British was that taken by the *Emden,* through the Dutch East Indies, but once inside this huge ocean, surrounded by enemies, how was the *Emden* to survive?

Captain von Müller had no false hopes about surviving forever. He intended to live as a cannibal, off the captives of the *Emden.* The captives would supply her with coal and with food and clothing. As long as she could evade the hundred warships that the British could bring to bear against her she could survive. Von Müller knew that when he took the *Emden* through the Strait of Lombok he was steaming into a trap; huge as it might be, the Indian Ocean was still a cage to him and his points of exit were few and easily guarded. Von Müller, however, gave no thought to points of

exit. His problem was to effect an entry without being discovered and chased.

The first item in his plan was to find that right entry, and
the one he chose, between Lombok Island and Bali, took him
through waters that saw little shipping. Von Müller also
timed their arrival so they could pass through the strait at
night. Leutnant von Guerard had been listening to the Dutch
traffic on the wireless and from the liveliness of the communication, even though it was in secret code, von Müller was
certain that the Dutch were increasing their watchfulness.
He did not wish to be seen, for he expected that the Dutch
would announce his presence in the area to the world after
the *Tromp* incident, and if he were placed south of there it
would be apparent that he had slipped into the Indian
Ocean.

The *Emden* and the *Markomannia* steamed slowly among
the lesser islands all day, taking care that no masthead came
in sight above the horizon. As they whiled away the day,
First Officer von Mücke worrying about the problem of
secrecy, came forth with an inspiration. The *Emden* was
easily recognizable as a German light cruiser by her size,
shape, number, and placement of guns, and her three funnels. British light cruisers carried four funnels, and there
were no light cruisers of other nations in this area. So
wherever she might go, the three stacks of the *Emden* would
be her trademark, and every spy in the Indian Ocean could
spot her the moment she appeared. Why not, then, make her
look like a British cruiser? All it took was the creation of
another funnel. Von Mücke took his idea to the captain, and
the captain approved.

It was afternoon. There was not much time to do the job,
but von Mücke improvised expertly. He mustered a detach-

ment of men and sent them below to bring up a supply of deck runners, strips of canvas about six feet wide which were used to protect the linoleum deck during coaling.

On deck a large wooden post was fastened to the planking in front of the forward funnel, and the deck runners were rigged around it to look like another funnel. From the side it was most impressive. From head on the framework left something to be desired, since it was skinny and badly proportioned, but passing through the straits they expected viewers to look at them from the side and not head on. The captain said it would do.

In the evening the round red sun came down to the sea and plunged below the horizon, as it does in the tropics, bringing darkness very quickly. The *Emden* had been loitering near the entrance to the strait until the last rays of red gold faded from the sky, and even later. It was ten o'clock that night before she began her passage through the narrow waters. She met one steamer and several sailing ships in the passage, but none of them came near or showed any particular interest in her. Still, before the passage was completed at midnight the crew in the wireless room heard Radio Batavia announce that a four-funneled "torpedo boat" had been seen in the area.

On the morning of August 29, First Officer von Mücke suggested that he could build a really effective funnel which would be collapsible and could be used whenever the *Emden* wished to conceal her identity. Captain von Müller gave permission, so the first officer set to work. He brought up lathing and more sailcloth. He knew that the British cruiser *Yarmouth* carried three round funnels and one oval one, and he decided that the *Emden* would emulate this style. In half a day he had constructed a most presentable funnel.

The funnel was rigged with wire-rope stays that were fastened to the foremast, and these were marked so that the same position could be attained each time the canvas rig was was to be hoisted.

For the next few days the *Emden* and the *Markomannia* steamed along the southern and western coasts of Java and Sumatra, moving at about twelve knots, staying always around sixty to seventy miles outside in order to avoid the curious. Captain von Müller expected a quiet time, and he had it.

The first of September came. Fresh food grew very short and was rationed to the men, who had to do the physical labor, while the officers began to live on canned meats. It was discovered in the officers' mess that they had a huge supply of paté de foie gras, which was welcomed in the beginning, but soon palled as a staple.

On the afternoon of September 3 the *Emden* approached the island of Simalur, which lies off the coast of Sumatra. Captain von Müller intended to move into the harbor of Langini and coal there the following day. He did not wish to run at night, so the *Emden* spent the night cruising slowly back and forth well outside. Had she arrived twenty-four hours earlier she would have lain helpless in the bay, engaged in coaling, as the English warship *Hampshire* came into the harbor to search. Even that night the English ship lay off the southern coast of Simalur at anchor.

On the following morning, the *Emden* and her coaler moved into the narrow neck of Langini Bay. It was an admirable spot for coaling. Inside the bay stood a small island, and behind that island a ship could anchor and no one outside could see any sign of life, and behind this was a chain of smaller islands with a deep channel running around them. The *Emden* came from the east and moved in from the north to Langini Bay without ever knowing how close she had passed to an enemy large enough to destroy her.

At nine o'clock in the morning the tiresome task of coaling began again. The *Emden* could take on a thousand tons, including the extra loads for deck and the rear of the forecastle, but there was time only to load a few tons before the heat became oppressive and the captain ordered the coaling stopped. After lunch and a rest it was begun again, but it went dreadfully slowly.

In the afternoon, as the coaling began again, a few lucky men and officers sat on deck, amusing themselves by watching the birds and the natives on shore. Obermaschinist Berglin, a specialist who had no part in the coaling, sat on the poop deck with a fishing rod in hand and soon had a number of handsome large fish in a pile at his feet. Dr. Schwabe, the enthusiastic young surgeon, decided that he would try his hand at fishing and borrowed a pole and line. He fished mightily for an hour, without much luck, and then was forced to go below for a few moments, leaving his line in the water. While he was gone, Leutnant von Levetzow was seen to loiter near the doctor's fishing place, and when the doctor returned, suddenly he had a huge fish on the line. He reeled in and puffed mightily to make his catch, and when the hook and its burden broke water he saw it: an old boot, one of von Levetzow's finest.

As the doctor reeled in, von Levetzow had gathered the other officers around to see the fun, and when the prize was revealed in all its elegance, the crowd began to roar with laughter. The doctor endeared himself to everyone aboard that day, for once his moment of chagrin had passed he laughed more heartily than anyone else.

Toward evening the natives on shore became convinced that the men of the *Emden* and the *Markomannia* meant them no harm, so curiosity took over and they came out to the ships in tiny dugout canoes. Those who had sailed in the Polynesian Islands were contemptuous of the canoes of these Melanesians—they were poor things, dug out of logs, and they lay so low in the water and were so poorly balanced that one crew member sat with a coconut shell in hand with the single responsibility of bailing lest the canoe be swamped in the clear, flat, windless bay.

The natives were dark-brown people, stringy with muscle, and they wore nothing more than small cloth or bark loincloths. They brought coconuts and oysters. Dr. Schwabe let the men have the coconuts, but he forbade them to eat the oysters of these hot seas. They also brought fish, pineapples, and bananas. The men could have the fruit, but the fish too was forbidden, since the doctor took one look at the filthy hands of the natives on board and began muttering about communicable diseases.

For this food the natives would not take money, but they were delighted to have old bottles, boxes, and cigarette tins and went off happily, several of them holding bottles underwater until they were filled and then pouring them out with shouts of laughter.

The work of coaling was so very slow that it was continued until eleven o'clock that night, and still the bunkers of the *Emden* were not filled. They had drawn so heavily on the *Markomannia* in the last few weeks that her remaining supply of coal was deep in the airless hold, and with every will the men could not move at half speed in the intense heat and humidity.

They would have continued to work all night if necessary,

but the captain took pity on them and called a halt until morning. So all the hammocks were brought above decks, and surrounded by hordes of mosquitoes the exhausted men tried to sleep.

That night Prince Franz Joseph and his roommate, Leutnant S. Schall, went to sleep in the wardroom. Their cabin was on the lower deck and it was far too hot for the tropics and far too inaccessible in case of an alarm, so the pair had permission to change their quarters. The prince slept in a hammock and Schall slept on a mattress beneath him.

At about three o'clock in the morning the prince was awakened by an unearthly noise. It was repeated and he realized it was the ship's cat, somewhere beneath him, miaowing as if devils were in pursuit of her. He cursed the cat and his luck, and lay down to sleep again. The noise was repeated and repeated again. He sat up and tried to find a match in his trousers pocket. He fumbled, then discovered one and lighted it, grumbling because he had to go to the trouble while the confounded Schall lay there, much closer to the cat, without moving a muscle.

Match in hand, the prince looked down and began to laugh. Beneath him the half-naked lieutenant lay on his back, snoring, and between his legs lay the ship's cat and four kittens who had just come into the world.

At six o'clock the bells rang and the fifes blew and the men arose for a drink of cold tea and to begin coaling once again.

Having been in harbor for nearly twenty-four hours, the captain was certain that the *Emden* had escaped detection. This meant that he had evaded the Dutch ruling which provided that a warship could call at one of her ports only once in three months. In case of need, then, he could seek refuge in a Dutch East Indian harbor.

It was a pleasant daydream, but at eight o'clock it turned out to be no more than that, because at that hour a lookout in the crow's-nest reported a white pilot boat approaching, flying the Dutch flag. A few minutes later the little boat reached the harbor and anchored alongside the *Emden,* and the government officer came aboard.

When had the *Emden* arrived? he asked.

About nine o'clock on the previous day, the captain said.

The Dutchman laughed. Not exactly, he said. They had seen her turn into the harbor before seven that morning. The *Emden* would have to leave immediately, he said. She had already overstayed her twenty-four hour leave.

Von Müller said they could not leave, and indeed it was impossible, for the coaling was still in progress. So the Dutchman went down to the engine room and asked Chief Engineer Ellenbroek how long it would take him to get up steam. The engineer had steam ready for an emergency departure, but thought for a moment and said it would take him at least two hours to make ready.

So the smiling Dutch officer went back to the wardroom and sat, chatting, with the officers and men over whiskey and soda until eleven o'clock, while the sweating men of the *Emden* finished the coaling. The Dutch patrol vessel followed them for an hour as Captain von Müller traveled southeast, in the exact opposite of the direction he intended to go. Then the *Emden* turned, through a heavy cloud layer, and made a graceful sweep around to reverse her course. The destination was the steamer lane that ran between Khota Raja at the north end of Sumatra, almost due west to Ceylon, and around that island to Colombo.

8. ACTION: SEPTEMBER 7-21

ON THE morning of September 7 the *Emden* reached the east-west steamer route to Colombo and began steaming west. The lookouts were alert and ready to sing out at the first sign of an object on the horizon. Now the *Emden* was seeking action rather than avoiding it. She was ready to do battle with any ship of lesser magnitude than a heavy cruiser and would avoid that or a squadron only because they could sink her while staying out of range of her guns.

Already she and the cruiser squadron were accomplishing their purpose. Admiral Jerram was searching the seas for the German East Asia Squadron, so far without success. His intelligence officers would puzzle in the days to come over the whereabouts of the squadron and over the reports that the *Yarmouth* was being seen in two different areas at the same time.

Half a dozen times that day the eager lookouts sighted smoke and the *Emden* turned and quickened her pace, only to have the smoke turn into a low-lying cloud.

There was nothing to be seen on September 7 but sun and sea and sky.

Captain von Müller sat in his chart room and conferred with Navigator Gropius. The intersection of the east-west steamer route that led to Singapore and the Colombo-Rangoon route lay a day's sailing north of them, so he ordered Gropius to set a new course and the next day they were there.

September 8: nothing. All day long the *Emden* moved toward the intersection of the steamer routes, without success. In disgust the captain talked in the afternoon of finding the Colombo-Calcutta line and following it north. That night they headed northwest.

At eleven o'clock that night the foremast lookout reported a light four points off the starboard bow, and the welcome cry to clear the ship for battle rang from the bridge.

With his night glasses, Captain von Müller strained toward the light. It was the after running light of a ship, but what kind of a ship he could not tell. He ordered full speed and the *Emden* leaped ahead, the *Markomannia* laboring after her at fourteen knots but falling rapidly behind as the *Emden* hit twenty knots. Looking up, von Müller was displeased to see a shower of sparks and a black cloud of smoke coming from the stacks. In their eagerness the stokers were piling on too much coal too fast and making smoke instead of speed. The captain wanted to surprise his quarry, not announce his presence to the world. He made a note to discuss the matter with the engineering officer at the first opportunity. If this was a warship he had already given a warning that might decide the course of the battle.

But it was not a warship, as he could make out shortly through the night glasses. It was a single-funneled merchantman, traveling away from him. He told Gaede to put a shot or two over her bows, and the gunnery officer moved his crews into action. Two shots rang out, two projectiles moved across the merchantman, and then the Morse lamps were flickering.

The message was in English: "Stop your engines. Don't use the wireless."

The merchant ship obeyed.

The doughty Lauterbach had already won his position as prize officer, partly because of his excellent command of English, and he rounded up his prize crew. It included a wireless operator, a Morse signalman, helmsmen, engineers, and seamen—all the men it would take to run a ship if necessary. They were armed to the teeth. Lauterbach carried a pistol at his hip and in his belt a dirk. The others carried guns and pistols.

A cutter was put over the side and they stepped into it and were rowed to the merchantman. Now the *Emden* came close alongside, and the captain and the first officer stood on the bridge nervously waiting for Lauterbach's report.

Lauterbach puffed up the rope ladder that was flung over the greasy side of the merchantman and jumped onto the rusty steel deck. He spoke to the captain in English.

"What ship is this?"

There was no answer.

He spoke in French. This time the little captain fingered his filthy hat and replied.

"Ah," he said. "A British cruiser."

"No," Lauterbach replied. "A German cruiser."

The captain blanched and pleaded that his was a Greek merchantman. He was a neutral, he said.

Lauterbach demanded to see his papers and his bills of

lading. The captain tried to lie his way out. He said he was bound from Calcutta to Karachi, carrying coal. The papers were being sent by train.

Lauterbach knew he was lying and said so. The captain produced his ship's papers, and Lauterbach instructed the signalman to flash a message to the *Emden*.

"The Greek *Pontoporos*," blinked the light.

Captain von Müller and the crew were stirred with disappointment. Their first prize in the Bay of Bengal, and she turned out to be a neutral. But then Lauterbach's second message came. The captain had finally produced his bills of lading and charter.

"Carrying 6,500 tons of coal for the English government. On her way from Calcutta to Bombay."

This put a different light on matters. The neutral ship was carrying an unneutral cargo. It could be called war matériel and confiscated. Since it was coal there was no question about the interpretation the *Emden* would put on it. She needed coal more than her men needed food. The *Markomannia*'s bunkers were too nearly empty for comfort.

Von Müller signaled back that the Greek could consider herself captured because she had war matériel aboard. Lauterbach complied.

A few minutes later Lauterbach brought the captain of the *Pontoporos* over to the *Emden* to discuss his situation. It was a ticklish matter for the *Emden*, for while the cargo was English the ship was really neutral. It was resolved because the Greek captain agreed readily to change his charter and accept German money instead of British. He would be glad to work for the Germans, he said. It made no difference to him.

Now Lauterbach was sent back to the *Pontoporos* as prize

officer to take command of the ship. The armed guards were replaced by seamen who would supervise the operation of the Greek ship. Lauterbach on this trip also brought with him an English-language newspaper printed in Calcutta a few days before which carried a shipping-news column. He was able to point out on the chart the approximate positions of several merchantmen which had left port a few days earlier.

All day long on September 9 they moved toward the steamer lane. They expected to reach it on about September 11, and they had little hope of finding more prizes before then. But at nine o'clock on the morning of September 10 a lookout won his bottle of champagne when he spotted smoke on the horizon, and the *Emden* detached herself from her entourage to investigate. This was a proper prize, the S.S. *Indus*, a British merchantman.

The captain of the *Indus* supposed that the warship bearing down on him was a British cruiser. What else could it possibly be? So with the confidence of a yachtman asail on a private lake he ran up his Union Jack while the *Emden* was still far off and did the Germans the favor of identifying himself immediately.

Captain von Müller was still concerned with the niceties of sea warfare. There were distinctions and differences to be observed. She was an Englishman, this prize, but the condition of her charter was all-important. If she was carrying private goods it was one thing; if she was chartered by the British admiralty, it was another. If she was owned by the British government she was a warship. In the first case the ship might be liable as a prize but the cargo not, in the second the cargo might be a prize but the ship should be sent to port and sold off. In the third case the cargo could be confiscated and the ship sunk without question. War was considered to be a matter between governments, not between representatives of governments and individuals of the enemy power.

When the *Emden* came within easy range, the *Indus* placidly keeping to her course, the German ensign was hoisted suddenly and a warning shot went whizzing across the merchantman's bow.

The sea was calm, enough so that as the *Emden* came close alongside the British merchantman, Captain von Müller on the bridge could plainly hear the Englishman's response to the hail and warning not to try to use the wireless.

"Damned German," said the English captain in a voice that carried clearly between the two bridges.

Since Lauterbach was aboard the *Pontoporos,* Leutnant von Levetzow was sent to the *Indus* in charge of the boarding crew.

Vice-Steersman Meyer was the senior noncommissioned officer, and he armed himself to the teeth for the encounter with the hated enemy.

As the boarding crew descended into the cutter, they could not see the deck of the English ship, and the captain was otherwise occupied. But in the bowels of the *Emden* the engineering crew, looking through the lower portholes, could see papers burning as they fell to the sea. The Englishman was burning his code books and secret orders. It was to be expected.

This prize was a prize. She was a 3,400-ton passenger-freighter, en route from Calcutta to Bombay, chartered by the English government from the Indian government. She was an enemy no matter how one looked at her. Further, she was a military ship, for the condition of her charter held that she would be used to transport men and horses from Bombay to the European war front. Her decks were latticed with white-painted stalls for the horses. Best of all, because she was to embark troops for transport, the *Indus* was well-equipped with food and other supplies.

Captain von Müller now faced a new problem. Should he take the *Indus* into his train and search for a hidden harbor where he could transfer supplies? Or should he take what he could here in the middle of the ocean and then sink the enemy? He decided on the latter course because he was in the middle of a British lake, the chances of detection if anchored even in a deserted harbor were very great, and there was no possibility of sending the *Indus* as a prize to a friendly port. Within the Indian Ocean there was no friendly port.

Now an entirely new set of arrangements must be made. First, Lauterbach, the merchant captain, must be relieved of his job on the *Pontoporos*. He was the expert in the loading and movement of supplies. The navy men—warriors—found themselves now forced to depend on skills that were never taught in the maritime academy or on the training ships. To relieve Lauterbach, a new officer must be found for the *Pontoporos*, because the Greek captain was totally unreliable and Lauterbach half-expected him to try to flee at any moment. The mate of the *Markomannia*, a loyal German, was sent to the Greek steamer, and Vice-Steersman Meyer was detached from the boarding party to be head of the German armed guard on the ship. One of the cutters was sent to the *Pontoporos* to make these changes, and then both cutters were dispatched, one carrying Lauterbach, to begin what the sailors on the *Emden* called *sägen*—sawing. This process of unloading and loading on the high seas was to be repeated many times.

Lauterbach started up the rope ladder of the *Indus*, lost his footing, and, pistol at hip and dagger in belt, fell into the Bay of Bengal. He was fished out in a moment, sputtering and laughing, and was up the ladder this time with the skill of a trapeze artist, slightly shamefaced after this fall but ready to share the joke with all the others.

There was very little time for joking with Lauterbach about his mishap. His advice was needed about the unloading, and he fell to work immediately supervising the transfer of supplies.

There was enough soap to last the men of the *Emden* for six months. There was fresh meat and flour and all the other supplies they needed so badly at that moment.

Before the supplies were shipped, the English crew was taken, every man, from the *Indus* to the *Markomannia*. Kapitänleutnant Klöpper was sent to the *Markomannia*, too, with a military guard to be sure that the prisoners did not seize the *Emden*'s coaler and make off with her.

Then the cutters were ready to load and unload supplies. Captain von Müller maneuvered the *Emden* into a position in the middle of his three steamers. All the ships pivoted around the *Indus*, which lay stopped in the water.

All day long the boats scurried back and forth. By four o'clock in the afternoon the *Emden* had refurbished her lockers. A sinking party then boarded the *Indus*.

To speed the process of sinking, Gunnery Officer Gaede was told that he might use the English ship for a bit of target practice. He sent four shells into the ship. Still she did not seem to be inclined to sink rapidly. Captain von Müller did not want more ammunition wasted, so he told Gaede to stop, and then the vigil began. It took her an uncommonly long time to go down, even with her seacocks open and shellholes at the water line. She was an hour in listing heavily and then shipping water so that the bows sank. Finally she sank, gurgling. The air in her exploded and scattered debris, and the masts sprang out of the water and fell back onto the surface. Several boats were wrenched loose from their davits and lay floating.

The search for the next prize now began.

Beginning on the morning of September 11 the prizes began to come more rapidly. The *Lovat* was next, another English ship equipped to carry troops, also on her way to Bombay to pick up the Indian detachments destined for the war in France. Lauterbach was boarding officer. It was a little embarrassing, he told his fellow officers in the wardroom that evening, because the captain of the *Lovat* was an old friend of his from the days on the China coast. But war was war, and the captain was shipped, along with his crew, over to the *Markomannia* to await the discovery of a suitable *Lumpensammler,* or junkman, on which both crews could be placed.

From the *Lovat* Lauterbach had brought newspapers to the *Emden.* Captain von Müller was interested in them. He wished to see if his entry into the Indian Ocean had yet been discovered by the press. It had not.

There was good news. It came from the *Markomannia.* The captain of that ship had learned that three more merchantmen were under charter and were following directly behind the *Indus* and the *Lovat,* all bound for Bombay, all destined to carry troops to Europe.

Captain von Müller could not have asked for a more

effective intelligence report. All he need do was sit on the Calcutta-Colombo steamer route for a few more hours.

Transport number one showed up at ten o'clock that night, right on schedule. She was the *Kabinga*, 4,600 tons. But when Lauterbach boarded the *Kabinga* he discovered that the captain of the *Markomannia* had been misinformed. The *Kabinga* was laden with a cargo of jute and was bound for New York under charter to an American firm.

Here were complications. Captain von Müller could sink the *Kabinga*, because she was an English ship. But then Germany would have been bound to pay the American firm for the cargo. Von Müller did not wish to cost his government money, and he could use the *Kabinga* as a junkman, besides.

Lauterbach arranged affairs on the *Kabinga*, and the crews of the *Indus* and the *Lovat* were moved aboard that ship. She then joined the train. The *Emden* led now, followed by the *Markomannia*, then came the *Kabinga*, and last the poky *Pontoporos*. The convoy, when it kept together, was reduced to travel at nine knots.

Early in the morning of September 12 the *Emden* dashed off from her charges, awakening the men to action stations as she ran. Lieutenant Franz Joseph von Hohenzollern, the prince, rubbed the sleep from his eyes as he stumbled from his hammock in the wardroom and into his trousers, then groped his way down the passage and the companionway to the torpedo flat two decks below. There he could see nothing and could hear only what the bridge chose to deliver as information through the speaking tube. For fifteen minutes he and his men stood, waiting, then the word came that it was another merchantman and there would be no action from the torpedo division. He came on deck to watch the show.

Again it was an English ship, but again it was not one of the promised transports. It was the *Killin,* a coaler, bearing 6,000 tons of Indian coal from Calcutta to Bombay.

The *Emden* had more Indian coal than she wanted. Captain von Müller decided to sink the *Killin* without delay. The ship's company was informed, and the cutters began their work in the rising seas, carrying the men and the few possessions they were allowed to take with them from the coaler to the *Kabinga,* which came lumbering up with the other ships of the train. The sinking party did its work on the *Killin,* with more speed and more accuracy than before. The shells that were fired into her were better placed, and she went down in a very few minutes.

In midmorning the *Emden* sighted another ship, which turned out to be the *Diplomat,* a 7,600-ton vessel carrying a thousand tons of tea from Calcutta to London.

There was nothing here for the *Emden* and so the *Diplomat,* too, was to be sunk without delay. Captain von Müller was less than pleased with the performance of his engineers and stokers in the past. This time he decided to use a different technique. The officers and crew of the *Diplomat* were moved to the *Kabinga,* while Oberleutnant Witthoeft, the first torpedo officer, went aboard the *Diplomat* with a crew from his division. They carried explosives. The captain had ordered Witthoeft to make sure that the *Diplomat* sank quickly and cleanly.

Witthoeft and his detachment opened the seacocks and laid their charges. They left the ship, and ten minutes later, after a series of small explosions, she went to the bottom.

All the officers of the *Emden* were eager to lead boarding parties. Prince Franz Joseph was promised that he and von Levetzow could take the next ship, but when she came she turned out to be an ally, or so it was officially. The ship was the Italian steamer *Loredano*.

Italy had joined Germany and the Austro-Hungarian Empire in the Triple Alliance before the beginning of the war. Through his two boarding officers, Captain von Müller asked this ally for a little help, since Italy was not yet in the war. He requested the captain to take the crews of the four British ships into Calcutta. It meant taking on some two hundred people in all, including the wife of the captain of the *Kabinga*.

The Italian refused. Franz Joseph conducted the negotiations in French, because he spoke no Italian and the Italian spoke no English. But the prince was not above a ruse.

What would the captain do if the *Emden* put all these crews in boats and turned them adrift?

The captain would pick them up, of course.

So it was arranged, but by this time Captain von Müller was annoyed and decided to keep the *Kabinga* as his dump ship. The captain of the *Loredano* was reminded of his neutrality, and he promised that he would do nothing to give away the position or the condition of the *Emden*. Then he steamed away toward Calcutta and the *Emden* moved off south, as long as the Italian ship was in sight. Captain von Müller changed course and headed northward, but off the steamship route from Calcutta to Colombo and onto that from Madras to Calcutta.

On September 14 Captain von Müller decided to lighten his load, abandoning the *Kabinga*. He realized that once he had done so he would reveal to the world the secret of the *Emden's* presence in the Indian Ocean and that the fourth funnel would be of little value in the future. But there was not much alternative. The supplies aboard the *Kabinga* were running low, and he was not in position to operate a seagoing prison camp. The extra ships slowed his passage and created dangers. The English would have to be sent off, no matter what new dangers this might cause for the *Emden*. The prize crew came away and the military guard returned to the *Emden* and the *Kabinga* was given her position. Then there was a brief delay. Another British merchantman was taken, the *Trabbock,* a 4,000-ton coaler which was in ballast, coming to Calcutta for coal, just as arrangements were being made to free the *Kabinga*. The crew of the new vessel joined the crowd on the dump ship and sailed away for Calcutta as Leutnant von Levetzow went to place the demolition charges in the coaler.

Half an hour later the lookouts reported a light on the starboard beam and the *Emden* turned. She hailed, but instead of stopping, the other ship increased her speed and turned to run. She ran, but the *Emden* ran faster and soon was in position to begin firing.

Shots were fired across the bow of the other ship; still she did not stop until one was placed very close by and she was told that the next shots would land on the ship itself. Then she hove to.

The captain hailed the ship, and from her bridge came the word that she was the *Clan Matheson,* on voyage from Southampton to Calcutta.

"English?" asked the *Emden*.

"British," came the firm reply. The captain was a Scot.

Captain von Müller had a good chuckle on his bridge over that remark. Lieutenant Lauterbach had a far less pleasant time of it. When he went aboard the *Clan Matheson* he discovered she was carrying a load of Rolls-Royce automobiles, locomotives, typewriters, and other precision equipment of the kind to warm the heart of a man who loved the good life. She also had on board a racehorse destined for the stables of the Calcutta Racing Club and reportedly the favorite in the coming Calcutta Sweepstakes. There were other thoroughbreds aboard as well.

There was nothing to be done, however, except the usual, so Lauterbach reluctantly told the captain to shoot the horses, while the sinking crew did its work.

Captain von Müller now sought a deserted island with a good sound harbor. It was time to coal. The *Emden* had not taken time for coaling; the captures came so quickly. It was nine days since they had left the East Indies, and the cruiser's bunkers were running low. Von Müller always grew restless and testy when this was the case; now he sought deserted seas.

His decision to move off the steamer route came in good time. That night the *Emden* intercepted a message sent in clear by the Calcutta lightship for the information of all steamers. It gave the position of 86° 24′ east, 18° 1′ north, and reported that according to the Italian steamer *Loredano* the *Emden* had sunk the *Diplomat,* the *Kabinga,* and the *Pontoporos.* This message annoyed von Müller and infuriated his officers. The Italian captain had broken his word of honor!

The admiralty had no desire to frighten the wits out of British and Indian ships, so the news of the *Emden* was carefully kept an official matter for the moment. The naval station at Colombo was alerted and units of the British fleet began the search in earnest for the German raider.

On September 15, the *Emden* and her two steamers cruised slowly in a deserted region almost due south of Calcutta but well off the lines of travel. She would coal and then she would move discreetly away from the scene of these triumphs to another region.

The next day Captain von Müller decided to try coaling at sea. There was no suitable secret harbor in the area, and the sea was as calm as a lake at evening.

The *Pontoporos* was brought to the starboard side of the *Emden* and fenders and improvised fenders of washboards and hemp matting were placed between the two ships to reduce the friction damage. The *Emden* moved ahead slowly on her starboard engines and the *Pontoporos* stopped hers. Then the coaling began.

It was hot, but the men had grown used to that and to slow coaling because of it. There was no surprise in the heat. There was surprise when the two afterholds of the *Pontoporos* were opened and the officers looked down at the coal. The Chinese coal they had been burning came in large pieces and burned strongly. The Indian coal in this Greek ship was dusty and slack, and the engineer officers knew the moment they saw it that it would burn badly and smoke frightfully.

A few hours later, when the *Emden* began to burn the Greek's coal, Captain von Müller was too far away from the *Pontoporos* to recall his crew and sink the vessel. That might have been done had she remained, for the coal was even worse than it had looked. There was no more steaming without black smoke. The stokers must work twice as hard to keep the furnaces going, and the boiler tubes, which had been cleaned only once every ten days or two weeks, now must be cleaned thoroughly once a week.

On September 17 the *Emden* cruised in the upper Bay of Bengal.

All day long on September 18 the lookouts strained their

eyes but saw nothing until four o'clock that afternoon, when a smudge of smoke on the southern horizon was sighted. The captain saw no reason to waste coal chasing her, since she was heading north toward Rangoon, so the *Emden* changed course to intercept and came up with the merchant-man at nightfall. Lauterbach and his boarding party moved to the other ship and shortly made their report.

It was a disappointment. The ship was the *Dovre,* a Nor-wegian and a neutral. She was of no use to the *Emden* at all, unless she would take the crew of the *Clan Matheson.* For a price, the captain said he would do so. Von Müller gave him a hundred Mexican dollars and the captain was satisfied, since he would have to take them without pay if von Müller had insisted.

The crew of the *Clan Matheson* were very pleased with their prompt release and good treatment. As they were being transferred to the Norwegian, von Müller went aboard the ship himself and talked with the captain. He learned that the Norwegian had been scoured the night before by a warship's searchlight, although the warship neither stopped nor iden-tified herself. He also learned that the ship had come from Penang, Malaya, and that in harbor lay the French cruisers *Montcalm* and *Dupleix.* This last news made von Müller's eyes sparkle.

It was nearly dark when the *Emden* steamed away, south-ward, and the *Dovre* moved north to Rangoon. As the ships parted the erstwhile captives of the Germans gave three cheers for the enemy who had treated them so handsomely.

During his stay aboard the Norwegian, Lauterbach had picked up some recent newspapers from Penang. They told of the exploits of the *Emden,* or some of them, and they predicted that the German ship would be captured or sunk within a very few days. The officers laughed, but not too loudly. They knew, certainly, that they could not stay forever in the Indian Ocean aboard the *Emden* unless they went to the bottom with her. But they were also determined to remain afloat as long as possible and to wreak as much damage on British shipping as they could. So far they had captured or sunk nine ships. They wanted many more.

On September 19 the *Emden* took more coal from the *Markomannia* while at sea, since Captain von Müller learned that the British were searching for him in strength. From time to time the wireless calls of a ship that signed herself QMD were heard, and one night a shore station inadvertently told the *Emden* that this was the British heavy cruiser *Hampshire*. She was in these waters, and from time to time she came very close to the *Emden*'s course.

That night of September 19 the wireless transmission noises from QMD were so loud that von Guerard estimated the *Hampshire* was somewhere within ten miles of the *Emden,* but luckily the weather was dirty and the blacked-out *Emden* could not be seen.

In reading the newspapers Captain von Müller realized that the British were most concerned about the effect the presence of his ship would have on shipping in the region. He could also be sure that the British would not broadcast the facts of his victories, for the same reason. He decided that he wanted to frighten the people of the region just as much and as quickly as he could, and he came to the conclusion that the quickest way to make the *Emden*'s presence known to the most people was to stage a strike on a shore installation. For this publicity gesture he chose the important Indian city of Madras.

9. MADRAS

HE JOURNEY TO Madras occupied four full days of
steaming. It meant traveling straight across the Bay
of Bengal from Rangoon. In the middle of the voyage the *Emden* stood directly below Calcutta, and on September 22 she was as far from that city as she had been
when she lurked in the waters just off the capital of Burma.

The captain slowed his ship on the afternoon of September
22. He did not wish to arrive in Madras too soon, for it was
to be a night attack. The afternoon was spent bringing in
the hammocks and the awnings from the decks and stowing
them safely below, out of the reach of fire. The ammunition
in the turrets was doubled. The log was secreted in a place
off the bridge safe from shells.

Toward evening the *Markomannia* was detached, and a
rendezvous was made. She would be nothing but a hindrance
to the *Emden* in such an action and was best sent safely
away. They would meet again the next morning if the *Emden*
was successful.

At dark the fourth funnel was set. The *Emden* had made

sparing use of it in the Bay of Bengal, and no one was quite sure whether the enemy had discovered its use or not. In any event, with the fourth funnel attached the *Emden* did look like a British cruiser and there was a good chance that she could move almost onto the city without detection.

Madras expected anything but an attack—so much was apparent as the *Emden* steamed toward the city. The city spread along the beach for sixteen miles, inland for about eight miles. Throughout, Madras was as brightly lighted as in peacetime; the glow of the lights illuminated the shore clearly and could be seen very far out at sea. The harbor lights burned brightly, showing the installations and particularly the *Emden*'s target, the red-striped white tanks of the Burma Oil Company.

Around nine o'clock, as the ship steamed forward, the captain ordered the men to battle stations and the war watch was resumed. The *Emden* increased her speed and came in at seventeen knots. She still had reserves in case she needed them.

At nine-forty-five the ship reached a point about 2,500 yards off the beach and stopped. The ship's searchlights began to play, until one of them found the white oil tanks. The order was given to fire and the first salvo cracked out in the night over the starboard side. The first shells overshot the oil tanks and hit the battery on the other side in Fort St. George. But soon the gunners found their aim and flame began to spurt from the tanks. Other shots were fired into a steamer, and still others were sent into the city. In all, 125 rounds were fired. The oil tanks burned brightly, casting light across the city, to match the flashes of the guns on the *Emden*. The British manned their artillery, or part of it, but not a single shot fell closer to the *Emden* than a hundred yards, and most of the men on the ship did not even know that the British guns were firing at them.

Most of the harbor guns, however, were unmanned, perhaps because a large dinner was in progress at the Madras club that night, celebrating the news of yesterday: the announced sinking of Germany's one ship in Indian waters, the *Emden*. The celebrators were in the dining room when a servant padded in to call their attention to the fires burning brightly in the harbor and in the town.

The wind was blowing offshore that night, and this lucky fact probably saved half the town from burning. But as the *Emden* fired her last shot and turned north, the fires were burning brightly enough to suit the captain. He had expended all the ammunition he cared to on this target, and he felt that he had accomplished his purpose, brought surprise to the enemy and destruction to one of his major cities. For one lonely light cruiser this was no little accomplishment.

All night long the fires flamed in Madras. The crew of the *Emden* could see them as the ship reversed her course and turned south again, and when they were ninety miles out at sea the sky was still aglow.

The *Emden* steamed now past Pondicherry, the French colony south of Madras, hoping to find some ships at anchor there or in the harbor at Cuddalore, but there were none lying in the roads outside. The cruiser moved on to make its rendezvous with the *Markomannia,* then steamed ahead, eastward, apparently, to confuse any watchers ashore. Out of sight of land the ships turned south. The new destination was to be the water off the Ceylonese port of Colombo.

Captain von Müller faced two problems now: He knew that the enemy would be searching hotly for him, and he must find more coal—and this time good coal. On the trip south to Ceylon he considered coaling again from the *Markomannia,* but the seas were running high and there was no time to search for a landfall and a hidden harbor. He decided on the risk of running low on coal.

The plan was to steam around Ceylon, at a distance offshore of sixty to seventy miles so as to remain hidden from the land. On September 24 the *Emden* was moving south off the east coast of the island when von Guerard's wireless room intercepted a heavy flow of military traffic. Not long afterward other communications clearly indicated that a Japanese warship had passed them, about sixty miles off their port beam, sometime during the day. The hunt was drawing closer.

Sitting in the wardroom, the officers of the *Emden* talked of two matters. They wanted newspapers, to see what had happened in Madras, and they wanted good coal. At the moment they were using the Indian coal from the *Pontoporos,* and it smoked so much that they were constantly afraid of detection even at a distance of sixty miles from shore. The officers joked with Chief Engineer Ellenbroek about it; they said that every night when he said his prayers he asked God to send him a British ship from Europe, loaded with Cardiff's finest coal. Prince Franz Joseph even promised the chief engineer that in a few days they would find him such a ship and capture it.

On September 25 the *Emden* passed around the southern tip of Ceylon and moved inshore to a point twenty miles from the beach. The engine-room crew switched back to the good Shantung coal. It gave no smoke.

After lunch that day the ship approached the Colombo-Penang-Singapore steamer route, and very shortly afterward they sighted a smoke cloud ahead. Without increasing speed the *Emden* drew up on this ship, then hoisted her battle ensign.

The enemy was the *King Lud,* a 3,600-ton merchantman traveling in ballast from Suez to Calcutta. Except for some flour and potatoes, there was nothing of value on the ship— no coal to speak of and no newspapers of recent date. She was sunk without delay after the captain and crew were moved to the *Markomannia.* Supplies from the *King Lud* were also taken aboard the coaler, because she had housed so many foreign seamen that her food and other provisions were running low.

As darkness fell that night, the *Emden* lay thirty miles off Colombo, and the captain saw something that indicated to him the results of his Madras raid. Four searchlights stabbed out to sea from the naval base, guarding the entrance to the harbor. All night long they ranged back and forth. Colombo was not going to be surprised as Madras had been.

At nine o'clock that night the searchlights were six degrees off the starboard side when the lookouts sighted a light four degrees to port. The *Emden* gave chase, but when hailed in English as a precaution, the ship reported itself as the Norwegian tanker *Oceanis,* and the *Emden* dropped back without identifying herself. In these enemy waters, off the coast of the enemy's naval base, the captain did not wish to attract any attention, no matter how hungry he and his crew were for news of the effect of their exploit at Madras.

The *Emden* then turned toward the island of Minicoy, whose light was a guidon for ships coming east from Aden. At ten o'clock they saw a ship moving out of Colombo harbor, silhouetted time and again against the searchlights inside. For a time they steamed on a parallel course, then when the merchantman was well outside land they turned and hailed her. She was the English steamer *Tymeric,* carrying a cargo of sugar to England.

The *Tymeric* brought welcome news. In searching the ship Lauterbach discovered the newspapers he wanted, even that day's editions from Colombo, and the officers of the *Emden* were able to learn what damage they had caused and what fear they had brought in their raid on Madras.

The official government press report was terse and still informative:

"The German cruiser *Emden* appeared before Madras last night (Sept. 22) at nine o'clock and shelled the city. As a result of the first two salvos the gasoline storage tanks of the Burma Oil Company were set afire. Then the cruiser fired several more salvos, damaging a number of houses. The telegraph office was hit. A shore battery responded after the third salvo; the *Emden* ceased its fire then and retired. Two policemen on duty near the oil tanks were wounded. The steamer *Chupra* of the British India Company was in the battle zone, and eight of her crew were wounded. The principal result of this incident has been to stop the return of confidence of shipping men, of which the signs are already visible."

Captain von Müller's guess that a strike at a land installation would be valuable in destroying British morale was justified, and the officers of the *Emden* could even be generous to their unfriendly enemies. Captain Tulloch and his chief engineer were given playing cards to while away their time aboard the *Emden,* where they were still kept separated from the others, and several of the ship's officers found it possible to speak kindly to them in the euphoria of victory.

10. THE PARTING

wo DAYS later the prayers of Engineer Ellenbroek were answered. The *Emden* captured her Cardiff coal, 6,600 tons of it.

It came in the nick of time. Captain von Müller wanted to remain in the excellent hunting grounds around Colombo, but to do so he must have good hard coal that would burn without leaving a telltale smudge on the horizon. The *Markomannia*'s supply was very nearly exhausted. The *Emden* had last taken coal from her on September 19, before the attack on Madras, and by this time, six days later, Captain von Müller was again feeling the gnawing hunger for coal.

The newspapers captured aboard the *Tymeric* had a great deal more to say about the *Emden* than simply to describe her Madras adventure, and in the wardroom at midnight on September 25 the officers off duty were reading aloud to one another so that none should fail to be proud of their heroic exploits. That is how they were termed even in the enemy newspapers, and Captain von Müller was compared several times to a knight of the days of chivalry for his gentle treatment of the crews from the vessels he captured.

Even the advertising columns noted the exploits of the *Emden*: An advertisement for one brand of soap boasted "the soap is so good that even the *Emden* took it from the *Indus* and used it."

At one o'clock on the morning of September 26 the alarms sounded and the papers were put down and the officers rushed to battle stations. It was a merchantman again, not yet their coal ship, but the 4,000-ton ship *Gryfevale,* bound from Aden to Colombo in ballast. The crews of the *Tymeric* and the *King Lud* were considerably overloading the *Markomannia,* and Captain von Müller decided it was time to create another junkman which would house the prisoners captured in the next few days.

At three o'clock on the morning of September 27 the marvelous coal ship appeared out of a cloud of dense smoke. She was the *Buresk,* carrying coal for Admiral Jerram's ships from England to Hong Kong. She, too, was added to the *Emden's* retinue, and the next few hours saw frenzied boat activity among the ships of the little squadron. The transfers of crews to the *Gryfevale* were being made. All were transferred except a handful of Englishmen aboard the *Buresk,* who said they would remain with their ship even as prisoners of war rather than be shipped back to port as passengers.

So on September 27 as dawn deepened into morning the ships steamed across the calm sea under a clear sky. Nothing could have seemed more peaceful than the *Emden* leading her flock, the *Buresk* on her port side, the *Gryfevale* on the starboard, and the *Markomannia* behind the *Gryfevale.*

Aboard the *Emden* that day the officers were just sitting down to their lunch—soup, corned beef with rice, and stewed fruit—when the ship veered so sharply and increased speed so rapidly that the table moved on its gimbals and the water slopped in the glasses. The soup spilled over onto the tablecloths, but no one was there to mind, because the entire wardroom spilled out onto the quarterdeck to see what was happening.

It was another smoke cloud. For a few moments the captain hesitated before calling the ship to battle stations, then a single funnel showed, and the tension relaxed. Another merchantman.

This ship was the steamer *Ribera*, the *Emden*'s fourteenth capture since the beginning of the war and her thirteenth in less than three weeks. The *Ribera* was in ballast and had nothing to offer the *Emden* except fresh provisions to supplant the corned beef for a while, a complete British signal book, and the captain's information that the Germans would not find many more ships in the Indian Ocean. He had just learned by wireless, he said, of a port embargo of ships in the Bay of Bengal. No more were to sail from any port until the *Emden* was destroyed. Further, the captain reported, even if the government had removed its embargo the captures of the past fortnight and the bombardment of Madras had sent insurance rates in that area skyrocketing until it was prohibitive for a ship to sail.

The *Emden* was again cruising in the direction of Minicoy Island. Hunting was very good indeed, but it could not continue much longer. It was now eight days since the last coaling; the supply of smokeless coal was nearly gone, and Captain von Müller knew that the captures and sinkings of five ships in the past week would bring a flock of enemy warships to the area.

It was hard to disengage. At nightfall the *Emden* came

across the 4,000-ton steamer *Foyle,* removed the crew, and sank her.

The crew of the *Foyle* was added to the *Gryfevale,* making it impossible to stack another man in that ship. She was dispatched with instructions to sail on a certain course lest she be torpedoed by other German warships in the area. This warning was Captain von Müller's bluff, given to throw the British pursuers off his scent. He had the feeling that this area was becoming much too dangerous for him and was taking every possible precaution to avoid engagement with the British fleet. The *Gryfevale* steamed off on her prescribed course, and the men of the *Emden* were pleased and flattered to hear their enemies give three cheers for them as they sailed away.

Captain von Müller then ordered Navigator Gropius to set a course for the Maldive Islands. This little chain was off the beaten path, and the chance of the *Emden* encountering either an enemy or a prize was very slim.

The men needed a rest, and the ship needed coal and a chance to stop somewhere so that the bottom could be scraped. She could not manage her top speed now, even burning Shantung coal, for the resistance of the barnacles was too great.

No one spoke of it, but now, on September 28, not a man in the crew expected to see Germany again. Each night the atmosphere screeched with wireless messages, many in code but so many in clear that von Guerard could report an estimate that at least sixteen enemy ships were now in pursuit of the *Emden.*

Some were British, some were French and some were Japanese. Every one of these ships was more powerful than the *Emden;* each one outgunned her and could sink her in an even battle. The *Emden* relied for her life on stealth and speed—not even speed, except in flitting about her self-imposed prison in the Indian Ocean, for all these ships were not only heavier but faster than she.

The officers and men of the *Emden* were not discouraged; quite to the contrary they were uplifted by a patriotic zeal that made them proud of their position as raiders. They were among Germany's first heroes, and they knew it. They would sacrifice themselves, and by showing their willingness they were exhibiting the highest love of the fatherland.

All this feeling of impending martyrdom sat close beneath the surface. It served to buoy the men's spirits when they stood without sleep for twenty-four and forty-eight hours at a stretch. But somewhere there must be a breaking point, and on the capture of the *Foyle* it was nearly reached.

On September 28 as the *Emden* steamed toward the Maldives, the men rested. Except for clearing the ship to coal, most did nothing, and even the war watch was distinctly relaxed. Some simply collapsed in their hammocks. Others sat on deck and played with the ship's cats, Pontoporos, Lovat-Indus, Kabinga, King Lud, and Diplomat, the runt.

The runt was also called the little idiot by the officers, who took great pains to keep him from his chosen desire, which seemed to be to march overboard. The runt got lost. In the relaxation of the ship the kittens were sitting up on the poop, rolling and playing in the sun, when someone noticed that there were only three of them. The officers on "kitten-watch" assured their threatening fellows that the kitten could not have fallen overboard. A search of the ship was ordered and carried out, but no kitten appeared. The officers sat down to afternoon coffee, berating the careless ones, and even the afternoon band concert did not go as well as it should have. Then, on the evening watch, the kitten was found. He had fallen down from the poop, twenty feet into the rear magazine, and was discovered peacefully asleep in an ammunition box, sore in one hind leg but otherwise safe and sound. The ship could relax once again.

On the morning of September 29 the men were rested enough to begin the necessary coaling. At eleven o'clock the Maldives came in sight, and the *Emden* led the way through a tortuous series of passages until Captain von Müller was positive that they were out of sight of ships on the high sea. Coaling began at eleven and continued for twelve hours.

On the morning of September 30, the *Buresk* moved alongside the *Markomannia,* made fast, and took off her surplus of oil and water.

After lunch the *Emden* moved alongside the *Marko-mannia* to finish the job of coaling. By half-past-seven the cruiser was again loaded with a thousand tons of coal.

Zahlmeisterapplikant Bordeaux, one of the ship's clerks, went aboard the *Markomannia* to carry the mail and post it from a port in the East Indies. He also took fifty English pounds, to buy provisions. The *Markomannia* could not buy so much as to make her purchases obvious, of course, but some needs could be filled.

At eight-thirty that evening the *Markomannia* steamed away, followed by the cheers of the men of the *Emden* for her safe journey. The plan was laid: They would meet again at the beginning of November at a designated rendezvous. Many brave words were spoken that night, but aboard the *Emden* few really believed they would ever meet their friends of the *Markomannia* again.

11. ACTION: OCTOBER 1-20

T HE *Emden* needed a good week in drydock, but since this was impossible in the midst of enemy waters, Captain von Müller sought a deserted coast where she could be run in and canted so her barnacles could be scraped, and where there would be no ships to chase them or be chased, and the engineers could do their work.

The cruiser moved slowly south, the engine-room crew doing as much repair work as possible while at sea. On October 3 the ship reached the Chagos Archipelago, and she began moving slowly among the islands, anchoring here and there. The tubes in the boilers were changed. Only four of her boilers were in use at any time; the others were under work. The engines were stopped alternately and the machinery was repaired and cleaned. The condensers were overhauled and the salt scraped off.

On October 9 all was done that could be done without canting the ship so that the bottom could be exposed and the bottom and sides could be painted. At seven o'clock that morning Captain von Müller ran his ship and the coaler,

Buresk, into the harbor at Diego Garcia, the southernmost of the islands. He chose this little bay because it was surrounded by high ground and could not be seen from the waters outside.

The *Emden* and the *Buresk* made ready to coal. Arrangements were completed, the fenders were hung, and the coaling from the *Buresk* began. At the same time some of the watertight compartments in the *Emden* were opened and filled on the opposite side of the ship and the *Emden* was thus canted, to starboard and then to port. As she was canted crews swarmed over the sides and scraped the barnacles, then scrubbed the sides and bottom as far as they could reach, and repainted her, below the waterline with rust protector and above with their gray hull paint.

This task and the coaling took all the rest of the day until midnight, and then was renewed again in the morning.

It was October 10, and they had spent ten days out of action. It was time to return to the shipping lanes. At eleven that morning the two ships moved out of the tiny harbor and began to cruise northwest on their decoy run. Out of sight of land they changed to a northeast course, cutting in and out of the Aden-Australia shipping lane. The captain of the *Ribera* had volunteered the information that hunting for troopships ought to be good in this territory. What they would do with the troops if they captured a shipload of them was never determined, because they saw no signs of shipping.

The *Emden* stopped briefly in the Maldives to take on the maximum load of coal from the *Buresk,* and then the *Emden* was ready once again to become the terror of the Indian Ocean.

On October 15 they captured the *Clan Grant.* She carried a mishmash of goods, including live cattle, and—wonder of wonders—prodigious supplies of beer and cigarettes. The cattle were shipped aboard the *Emden* and her transport, and 250,000 cigarettes were brought aboard the *Emden*. The ship now had a definite barnyard smell about it. Besides the cows, for whom the carpenters built stalls on the middle deck, there were the grunting pigs and the cackling chickens, each adding its bit to the effluvia. When the ship was in motion all was well, but when she was stopped on the windless sea it was another matter.

Taking part of his cargo, First Officer von Mücke returned to the *Emden* leaving Lauterbach and one of the young lieutenants from the *Emden,* Leutnant Fikentscher, in charge of the prize crew. The *Clan Grant* would be kept with them for a short time, until she was emptied of the valuables.

It was Lauterbach's sorry duty to report to the captain of the *Clan Grant* that his ship would be stripped and then sunk, sorry because the captain was an old China hand and Lauterbach had seen his scrubby beard and broad beam in many a port before. They were, in fact, old friends of years' standing.

That following day, October 16, the *Emden* sent seventeen men aboard the merchantman to clean her out of supplies that could be used. The *Emden* replaced her crockery and table linen, and the engineering department got firebricks in quantity. The cigarettes and beer came out by the caseload.

The unloading was proceeding, even though there was a heavy swell that day, when a smoke smudge came up on the horizon. Captain von Müller trained his glasses on it and recalled Lauterbach from the merchantman for more prize duty.

The *Emden* raced toward the smoke. As the silhouette became clear the captain was puzzled. It did not look like a merchantman. Perhaps it was a new model of destroyer. He ordered the crew to battle stations.

The tension grew until the *Emden* closed with the other ship, and suddenly seeing it broadside on, it was apparent from the bridge that they had wasted their adrenalin on an ocean-going dredger.

The men from the dredger went to the *Buresk* and the *Emden* went back to ransacking the *Clan Grant* until Captain von Müller declared an end to it and the ship was sunk. The rest of the day remained quiet until just before midnight when the *Emden* came up on the 4,800-ton steamer *Ben Mohr,* loaded with machinery. The captain had the crew removed and sank her at once.

October 17 and 18 were quiet days, with no sightings except a Spanish mail packet, which the *Emden* turned to avoid. It was apparent that the port officials at Colombo suspected their presence in the area if they could not confirm it, and shipping was either being diverted or stopped.

On Sunday, October 19, the captain decided to try the Colombo-Bombay shipping route, and that afternoon they took the Blue Funnel liner *Troilus,* which was also carrying an extremely valuable cargo of metals and rubber destined for England and the war effort.

The captain of the *Troilus* was furious, and in his anger he revealed a valuable military secret. The Colombo-Aden traffic had not been stopped, but had been routed thirty miles north of the usual lane. The *Emden,* in moving, had just happened to catch the *Troilus* on her way.

With the capture of the *Troilus,* the *Emden* embarked on a period of swift action and great complications. The news that the steamer lanes had been changed caused Captain von Müller to take the *Troilus* into the train for the moment.

He did not wish to waste daylight hours in transferring passengers and crew and in sinking her. Besides the *Buresk* was now very full, and something must be done to get the men off her. He would not send the *Troilus,* with its valuable cargo of war matériel, back to port as a dump ship, and he had no time to dump the cargo, even if his men had been able to do so.

The simple solution was to capture another passenger freighter, preferably in ballast, and send the noncombatants to safety in her. So the scouring began.

That evening the *Emden* found just what she wanted: the English steamer *St. Egbert,* carrying a cargo to New York— British ship, neutral cargo. There was their new junkman.

Now the captures followed so quickly that there was no time for changing the guard. Lauterbach was left aboard the *Troilus* for the moment. Prince Franz Joseph and Leutnant Levetzow were selected to be the next boarders, because still another boarding crew was on the *St. Egbert.* Anyone could now see why Captain von Müller had taken so many extra men aboard the *Emden* in Tsingtao and in the South Seas. Fourteen men had already left the *Emden* aboard the *Pontoporos;* one was on the *Markomannia;* sixteen were aboard the *Buresk;* and now two steamers were in the train, each with a prize crew of a dozen officers and men aboard, and still another prize crew must be formed.

Shortly after midnight the *Emden* captured the third steamer of the day. She was the *Exford,* carrying coal. Captain von Müller could not pass up the coal, so this ship was added to the little fleet. It was a rough night and a troublesome one for the men of the *Emden.* The prince, aboard the *Exford,* found it difficult to keep up with the *Emden.* Leutnant Geerdes, aboard the *St. Egbert,* misunderstood instructions, turned north-northeast instead of northwest, and was out of sight for many anxious hours. He stopped the ship and hove to; then, when the seas slackened, he moved back to the course and tried to find the impromptu convoy. Luckily the captain had considered what might have happened, and he stopped the convoy early on the morning of October 19 so the *St. Egbert* could catch up. She did, but not until seven in the morning. He went out and found her, leaving Lauterbach on the *Troilus* in command of the flotilla.

This day, October 19, was as busy and confusing as any day in the *Emden*'s voyage. It began with the transfer of the various ship's crews from the captured vessels to the *St. Egbert*. From the *Buresk,* German boat crews were needed to ship supplies for the use of that coaler and to ship extra supplies aboard the *St. Egbert* for the civilians.

Boats from the *Buresk*, the *St. Egbert,* the *Exford,* and the *Emden* ranged around the two condemned supply ships, carrying off the loot. Finally the confusion sorted itself out, and the captain ordered all boats clear of the *Troilus.* Gunnery Officer Gaede put several shots into the ship at the water line.

It was after dark when the job had been done and the false course had been taken and corrected, and the *Emden* was again steaming where she wanted to go, southward now.

The captain lay back in his easy chair on the bridge and announced that no matter what came in sight, except a warship, he was not to be disturbed. They were not capturing any more ships until the morning. It had been a very trying day.

12. ATTACK

THE SOUTHERN course set that weary evening of October 19 soon gave way to new settings: south-southeast, and then southeast, and later it would be due east. The *Emden* was headed toward a goal. She would steam into Penang harbor on the eastern coast of the Malay Peninsula and attack the warships anchored there.

All was quiet on October 23, 24, and 25, quite intentionally. The captain wanted as much rest for himself and his men as he could obtain. Their next objective was the most difficult they had attempted. Singlehandedly they would dash into the harbor of the enemy, select a target, fire, and attempt to dash out again without being destroyed. No one knew what they would find in Penang harbor, except that von Müller was quite certain it was being used as a base for warships. He might find the *Montcalm* and the *Dupleix* there, both larger than the *Emden*. In fact, nearly any cruiser he might find would be larger, faster, and more heavily armed than his own ship.

On October 26 the *Emden* and the *Buresk* pulled into

Nancowrie harbor in the Nicobar Islands, which lie northwest of the northern tip of Sumatra. It was time again to
coal. For the first time since war had begun the decks were
cleared of coal. Captain von Müller made sure that no extra
fire hazard would be available as a target for enemy guns.
As the coaling ended, the name and port of the *Buresk* were
painted out, and she was sent to the rendezvous west of Sumatra to await the coming of the *Emden*. Kapitänleutnant
Gropius, the *Emden*'s navigator, was left aboard as captain
of the ship. Von Müller wanted no slip-ups where his coal
supply was concerned.

On the evening of October 26 the *Emden* set her course
for Penang harbor and steamed slightly faster than she had
been able to move with her coalers, at twelve knots. Early on
the morning of October 27 that speed was increased to fifteen knots. The object was to come to the lip of the harbor
just before dawn of the next morning and to dash in and
make the attack at dawn.

At eight o'clock that night the *Emden*'s speed was increased to seventeen knots and the fourth funnel was hoisted
into place. The captain remained on his bridge examining
charts of Penang harbor.

The harbor lay between the sandy coast of the Malay
Peninsula, on the east side, and the island of Pulo-Penang
on the west. There were two openings, one to the south and
one to the north, but the southern opening was too shallow
for oceangoing vessels; thus as far as the *Emden* was concerned the harbor was inside a bottleneck formed by the
channel, which was a thousand yards wide. The *Emden* must
move around the north side of Pulo-Penang Island and close
in to avoid beaching on the sandy Malay coast. The port facilities were located on the island, in and around the town

of Georgetown. The course for the *Emden* was simple and clear. She must run in very close to the island, at high speed, with her helm hard astarboard as she rounded the point, and then Captain von Müller must be prepared to take in the situation in the harbor at a glance and decide in a few seconds how to make his attack. All depended on what he found in the harbor. He expected to find it dotted with merchantmen, but he was not seeking merchantmen this time. He must spy out the warships immediately, head for one of them, loose his torpedoes and gunfire, sweep around, and charge out of the harbor. The greatest danger was that a torpedo boat might be lurking near the edge of the harbor or might be able to reach the bottleneck before he could make his sweep and emerge. Then the *Emden* would be a clear target for a torpedo. But that was unavoidable, the known risk he must run.

At midnight the ship went on full war watch. Two hours later the lights of Penang came into view. The captain ordered the ship slowed and she cruised at eleven knots back and forth, out of sight of the harbor in her darkness. They saw a steamer enter the harbor and stop near the brightly lighted buoy, apparently waiting for the pilot. Still they waited, moving nervously back and forth outside.

The moon went down. At four-thirty the officers were warned to be ready for action and the *Emden* turned toward the harbor mouth. She passed a small island near the opening of the bottleneck, and saw a pilot boat a few yards abeam. The boat was heading for the stopped steamer and paid no attention to the four-funneled cruiser.

Just before entering the harbor, Captain von Müller reduced speed and looked around him. Even in the grayness the lights stood out. On the port side were four particularly bright lights, evenly spaced, that at first seemed to belong to houses on the far shore. But as the earliest golden rays of dawn appeared, the lights separated and disclosed large funnels and the superstructure of a warship.

Torpedo Officer Witthoeft shouted to the prince through the speaking tube to be sure the starboard torpedo tube was clear. He checked again, and reported. While the ship waited, Captain von Müller stopped the engines.

In these brief moments the dawn was breaking full, and now the officers and some of the men recognized the ship before them. It was the Russian light cruiser *Yemtschuk*. Oberleutnant Lauterbach knew her well. He had been the guest of her commander in Vladivostok harbor.

Captain von Müller ordered the engines started and moved toward the quiet enemy. The battle flags were run up the masts, declaring to the world the identity of the German ship, and she turned hard aport to bring the port torpedo tube to bear on the beam of the Russian cruiser. At five hundred yards, as the dawn broke from the bridge, the captain and the torpedo officer could see a steam pinnace pulling away from the Russian, toward the town of Georgetown. Captain von Müller stared at her for a moment, worrying lest she be a dreadful enemy herself. No. It was only the cookboat, bearing the petty officers and cooks who would go in early morning to the market to buy fresh supplies.

A few seconds and the *Emden* turned to port, and now her port torpedo tube was properly aimed. At three hundred yards, still without a stir from the cruiser, Torpedo Officer Witthoeft pulled the release handle and the torpedo leaped from the tube, its propeller whirring. It was five-eighteen when Witthoeft shouted:

"Torpedo los!"

On deck the men strained in the gathering light and could see the telltale track of bubbles. At the searchlights the crewmen waited for the order, but it never came—their lights were no longer needed; the enemy was in plain view and not more than 250 yards away.

Now there was stirring aboard the *Yemtschuk,* movement on the bridge and on the decks. It was too late.

A second passed, and then another. There was a muffled explosion, below the water line, and the *Yemtschuk* seemed to leap out of the water, a large splash appearing against her hull just below the second funnel. Then she fell back and settled as far as the flagstaff on the poop.

From the conning tower Witthoeft's muffled voice could be heard over the tube system in the torpedo flat, where nothing could be seen. The torpedo had struck, but had not finished off the ship. Another run was to be made.

As the torpedo splash was seen from the deck of the *Emden* the men began to cheer, but their first cheer was drowned by the thunder from the *Emden*'s guns, which opened on the Russian, aiming at her forecastle where the men were sleeping.

The bright blaze of the sunlight was joined now by blazes from the ship. She was afire, deep in the water, and the *Emden*'s shells were gouging into her.

Captain von Müller speeded around in a turn to port, to fire the starboard tube. In these few moments of maneuver the *Yemtschuk's* crew, or some of them, managed to move to action stations and some shells began to whistle across the decks of the *Emden*. Not far away from the Russian cruiser lay the French destroyer *d'Iberville.* She now opened fire on the *Emden* with her guns.

A few minutes' maneuvering and the ship was aimed and

the hiss on the bridge said the torpedo was away. First Officer von Mücke began to count: *"Eins . . . zwei . . . drei . . .
vier . . . fünf . . . sechs . . . sieb—"*

The torpedo exploded with a sharp crack, cutting him off
in midword. This second shot struck below the surface at a
point beneath the armored bridge and penetrated into the
torpedo storage of the cruiser. There was a second explosion,
and the center of the ship raised high, she broke into two
pieces and splashed back into the water.

Immediately smoke broke out, thick yellow, white, black,
and gray smoke laced with flickering tongues of flame. There
was a sizzling and a hissing in the water and a cloud spread
around and above the Russian cruiser.

Now the firing from the *d'Iberville* was very noticeable.
The firing from the *Yemtschuk* stopped, and the only action
that could be seen through the smoke was that of a handful
of survivors swimming in the bay.

The *Emden* could not stop to pick up survivors. She was
too closely hemmed in by the merchant ships in the harbor
and was under fire by the French destroyer. She turned
again, and as she turned the men of the *Emden* could see
what remained of the *Yemtschuk*. She was completely sunk;
only the tips of the masts projected from the water of the
harbor.

The captain considered the possibility of moving to deal
with the *d'Iberville*, which was screened from him by merchantmen. Then his attention was drawn to a ship approaching them at high speed from the mouth of the harbor, trailing
a dense cloud of black smoke of the kind that he associated
with the fast torpedo boats.

He turned hard aport and began running toward this new
enemy at maximum speed. At six thousand yards Gunnery

Officer Gaede opened fire on her with the *Emden*'s guns trained dead ahead. The boat turned and showed herself as a government pilot boat, quite harmless to the cruiser. She had received only one hit in the funnel, and that had not disabled her. The interruption had, however, caused the *Emden* to run so far out of the harbor that it was foolhardy now to turn back in and attack the *d'Iberville* or any of the twenty merchant ships lying at anchor.

The battle flags were hauled down as the *Emden* moved past the entrance buoy, and in a few moments the men were released from battle stations.

Not long afterward, First Officer von Mücke called the men aft and explained the progress of the battle to them. A few had seen the entire fight, but most of the men had seen at best a portion of it, and some, who served below decks, had not seen any of it, including the men in the torpedo division who had sent the deadly explosives into the Russian cruiser. The captain also came aft and reminded the jubilant men that the credit should go to the Kaiser for giving them the opportunity to serve him. They gave three cheers.

The ship settled down. The ammunition cases were cleared away and the guns were cleaned and reloaded. Breakfast was served.

At seven o'clock the ship was called again to action stations as smoke was sighted on the port horizon. At first the lookouts thought this vessel was an auxiliary cruiser, but she turned out to be an ordinary merchantman—not quite ordinary, because she flew the yellow flag that indicated a cargo of explosives. Lauterbach and the prize crew were sent to the ship, the *Glanturret*, to carry out the usual procedure. She would be sunk.

Lauterbach was talking to the captain when the signal

lamps from the *Emden* began to blink furiously. He was to deliver a message: Captain von Müller wanted to express his apologies to the men of the *Yemtschuk* for not stopping to pick up survivors and to the British pilot boat for firing on an unarmed craft. He had thought the pilot boat was a torpedo boat, he said, and he knew there were plenty of boats in the harbor to pick up survivors, so he had not remained.

The message was hardly delivered when Lauterbach's signalman was again at his side, telling the boarding officer that their orders were changed. The *Glanturret* was to be set free and they were to return immediately to the *Emden*. From the starboard an enemy was approaching at high speed and there would be another fight. There was no time to waste on merchantmen.

Lauterbach clambered back into his cutter and they rowed to the *Emden* to be hoisted on board. He tumbled out and ran to the bridge, for in the absence of Gropius he was the *Emden*'s navigator.

Less than five thousand yards from the enemy the *Emden* raised her battle flags, and the order came to begin firing. As they closed the *Emden*'s gunners began to shoot. The ship turned to port and the starboard guns were brought into action.

The enemy came ahead, then loosed two torpedoes and turned, presenting her beam as a target. The torpedoes passed harmlessly astern, and the *Emden* began to fire effectively. From the silhouette Captain von Müller could tell they were dealing with a destroyer, and from the tricolor streaming from her mast he could tell she was French.

The tricolor did not stream long. After two salvos the *Emden*'s gunners found the range and the third sent the flag dropping. One shell must have landed in the boiler room because white clouds of steam rose high above the ship.

The French manned their guns, particularly a machine gun forward of the conning tower, which sent bullets swarming above the *Emden*—like bees, some of the crew said.

At the end of the tenth salvo Captain von Müller ordered Gaede to cease fire. He was waiting to see if a white flag was run up from the badly holed ship.

No white flag showed.

Two more salvos were fired.

The eleventh struck home, and the firing aboard the French ship ceased. The twelfth also struck, and then the destroyer began to sink.

Captain von Müller ordered Lauterbach to move the *Emden* in closer. Lauterbach demurred. They were approaching very shallow water, he said, and if they went in much farther the *Emden* ran the danger of going aground.

Von Müller listened and agreed. They stood off and continued firing. At the end of the twentieth salvo the captain again ordered the firing stopped. The destroyer was down by the bows. Then her stern rose for a moment, and the entire ship disappeared.

The *Emden* moved in to about two hundred yards, going very slowly and sounding as she went. Lauterbach was careful not to lose the channel. Two of the cutters were put over the side, and in one of them Dr. Schwabe carried bandages and medicines to treat the survivors they could see swimming in the water.

It took a few moments longer to launch the second cutter, because as was customary before a fight the boat had been filled with water to keep it from catching fire if struck. The other, Lauterbach's cutter, had come back aboard too late for that treatment.

As the cutters approached, the French swam—but away from the boats, not toward them. They were afraid, the men of the *Emden* later learned, that they would be shot if the Germans picked them up. They preferred to take their chances in the sea, and one French sailor did actually swim all the way to Penang, but many of the survivors chose drowning rather than capture.

The *Emden*'s boats moved slowly through the water, picking up the wounded, who could not swim away. Then some of the sailors saw that they were not being murdered in the water and swam toward the boats. In all, thirty-six seamen and one officer were rescued and brought back to the *Emden*. The wounded were left in the boats while the unwounded climbed aboard the ship, and then the boats were hoisted on the davits amidship and the wounded were taken to the sick bay forward.

The unwounded Frenchmen were placed in the waist on the starboard side and were given an awning for protection against the sun. A few were questioned, and from them the captain learned that he had sunk the French destroyer *Mousquet*. He also learned that the destroyer had been on patrol duty at the north entrance to Penang harbor on the night before, but that she had ignored the *Emden* when she saw her approach because her captain saw the fourth funnel and was certain she was an English cruiser. When the French heard the noise of action in the harbor they had scurried in, passing the *Emden* on her way out, but again they had believed her to be an English ship and had paid no further attention. Even when the destroyer had seen the *Emden* later that morning they had thought she was an Englishman until the *Emden* opened fire on them. The captain, who had erred so badly in turning his broadside to the enemy, had distin-

guished himself at least by bravery. His legs had been shot
away in the fight, but he had had himself lashed to the bridge
and had gone down with his ship.

As the wounded were treated and the able-bodied were
made comfortable and given food and clothing from the
Emden's stores, Captain von Müller decided to move quickly
away from the vicinity. Two more French destroyers lay in
the harbor, he learned, the *d'Iberville,* with which he was
familiar, and the *Fronde*, of which he had been unaware because she was anchored some distance away from the Russian cruiser.

Leutnant von Guerard appeared on the bridge with wireless messages intercepted from the Penang station, reporting
the sinking of the *Yemtschuk* and the *Mousquet.* If any of
Admiral Jerram's cruisers were in these waters they would
soon be nearing Penang. The captain turned to Lauterbach
and ordered him to move out. The *Emden* began to steam
north at twenty-two knots, hoping to throw the enemy off
the track before turning south and west to join her coalers
at the Simalur rendezvous.

13. THE RING CLOSES

S THE *Emden* sped away from the scene of her triumph the messages from Penang continued to inform the allied fleets of her presence in the area. Captain von Müller was not long in discovering also that he was being followed by an enemy destroyer, which kept him in sight and most certainly kept Penang informed of his course and progress.

Lauterbach plotted the course west-northwest and the *Emden* steamed ahead. Around noon she plunged into a violent rain squall and in this cover changed course to northnorthwest. When the *Emden* emerged from the squall fifteen minutes later on the new course the destroyer was nowhere to be seen. The sea was clear and blue and the sun had never seemed to shine more brightly.

Captain von Müller decided that he would capture a ship and send the Frenchmen to safety in it. That would be his first mission. The *Emden* turned to the Penang-Rangoon shipping lane then and reduced speed to seventeen knots. She cruised along the ship lane until four o'clock in the afternoon, but found nothing. Then she turned west-southwest, but still found nothing.

Toward evening the port engines began running hot and Chief Engineer Ellenbroek asked for some time to stop them and repair them. Captain von Müller then sought the safety of the Nicobar Islands again. It would never do to have the *Emden* suffer any breakdown her own men could not repair, for there was no port at all to which she could turn for assistance. Breakdown meant disaster.

She ran into St. George Channel between Great Nicobar and Little Nicobar Islands, and the port engines were stopped while she cruised very slowly on the starboard power plants. The French prisoners were worried when the high wooded coasts came into view. They were afraid that they would be abandoned on these lonely islands to take their chances of survival and rescue, and it was necessary for the officers of the *Emden* to reassure them that this was not the captain's intent.

Despite the attentions of Dr. Luther and Dr. Schwabe, two of the most seriously wounded Frenchmen died during the night of October 28. The following morning at eight o'clock they were buried at sea with full military honors.

That next day the doctors labored over the other wounded and the captain searched vainly for a merchantman. None was found. On the night of October 29 another Frenchman died.

Early on the morning of October 30 the *Emden* captured a 3,000-ton freighter, the *Newburn,* carrying a cargo of salt to Singapore. Lauterbach went aboard and talked with the captain, who agreed readily to interrupt his voyage and take the Frenchman into Khota Raja, a nearby port on neutral Dutch Sumatra that was reported to have a modern hospital.

The French sailors were questioned about their intentions and were made to promise that they would not fight again against Germany in this war. They did promise, and the transfer of the healthy and the wounded began. Dr. Schwabe went aboard the *Newburn* and supervised arrangements on that end. Dr. Luther watched over the movement of the wounded from the *Emden*'s sick bay. The French officer, as he left, asked the prince if he might have one of the *Emden* hatbands as a memento, and it was given. The captain of the *Newburn* was given his course and told that by steady steaming he could be in Khota Raja by nightfall.

Then the *Emden* steamed away. By nine o'clock, when the last French sailor, the one who had died the night before, was given military burial, she had gone through the motions of setting the false course for the benefit of the *Newburn*, then changing to her true course, and she was running to the rendezvous where she hoped to find the *Buresk*. Coal was again the need.

The *Emden* met the *Buresk*, as planned, on the morning of October 31, and the two ships steamed slowly along the deserted western coast of Sumatra. Two days were given to cleanup and repair and rest. Promotions of various enlisted men were announced in a ceremony on the afterdeck, and later that day the officers were invited to the captain's cabin for a drink in celebration of their accomplishments.

November 2 was given over again to the dirty work of coaling. They had learned that they could not come inside the Dutch harbors to coal, and they had become quite expert at coaling on the high seas, so they undertook the process eight miles out, protected from the never-ending swell of the Indian Ocean to some extent by the land, but still well outside Dutch territorial waters.

The *Emden* parted from the *Buresk,* making a new rendezvous with her, and steamed into the Sunda Strait, which separates Java and Sumatra. After two days she had not encountered a single ship, so in disgust she turned away west toward the Cocos or Keeling Islands, where she was to meet the *Exford* and the *Buresk.*

On November 7 the *Emden* arrived at the rendezvous and the *Buresk* was there. The *Exford* was not. They searched all day and through the night for her.

All was well the next morning, when the *Exford* was found, fifty miles from where she ought to have been. The captain of the *Exford,* Kapitänleutnant Gropius, had seen a British convoy coming by and had changed his course.

Captain von Müller had a premonition that he was about to get into a fight. He wanted all his regular navy officers around him when it happened, so he began to exchange crews. The jolly Lauterbach, valuable as he was, was not regular navy but a merchant captain and he belonged aboard a merchantman, while Gropius, good a captain as he made, was a regular navy man who belonged back on the *Emden.* Much to Lauterbach's disappointment the captain ordered them to change positions, and Lauterbach took command of the *Exford,* buoyed up at the last by the captain's handshake and promise that they would meet again at a point a thousand miles west of the Cocos Islands in two to six days, and then he could return to the *Emden.* Leutnant Gyssling and Leutnant Schmidt, who had been in the *Buresk,* were brought back to the *Emden,* too. Then the *Exford* was detached, and the *Emden* and the *Buresk* steamed toward Direction Island, where the British maintained a wireless station and a cable relay station.

14. THE LANDING

ABOARD THE *Emden* on the night of November 8, Kapitänleutnant von Mücke made careful preparations for the next day's landing on Direction Island. So important a communications link deserved proper protection, and had the German position been reversed they would have stationed perhaps a hundred armed men on the island to repel attacks. That would be adequate protection against any single warship or any surface raider. No ship could afford to dispatch a landing force of more than fifty or sixty men, and an attacker would be reduced to shelling the installation from offshore. Effective as this might be temporarily, the destruction could be repaired rather quickly, and the important cables would be retained intact.

Since he must expect a vigorous defense of the island, von Mücke chose young but experienced men. The two officers he took with him, Leutnant Gyssling and Leutnant Schmidt, were well trained in infantry tactics. He chose thirty seamen, fifteen technicians, and two wireless men. Nearly all of them were nine-year men—sailors who had chosen to strike for petty officer and had elected to serve nine years in the navy, then would continue to make the navy their career.

Von Mücke commandeered all four of the *Emden*'s portable machine guns for the expedition. He would have taken more if they had been aboard. He also selected twenty-nine rifles and twenty-four revolvers. The men took the guns apart, cleaned them thoroughly, oiled them, and broke out new boxes of ammunition. The men laid out their whites, with boots or puttees, and they were issued helmets to shield their heads from the tropical sun.

That night the *Emden* lay fifty miles off the island. Early in the morning the fourth funnel was raised again and the ship began to steam toward its objective, hoping to take the wireless station quite by surprise and prevent any outburst of messages. The *Buresk* remained at the point where the *Emden* had lain. If all went well during the day she was to be called up for coaling after the destruction of the wireless station.

The *Emden* had been underway since well before dawn. By sunrise she lay outside the entrance to Port Refuge. At six o'clock First Officer von Mücke reported to the captain. He was ready to go ashore. He saluted, Captain von Müller returned the salute, and von Mücke stepped smartly off the bridge.

The two cutters were already in the water, and the officers and men of the landing party had already taken their places in the boats. The steam launch was ready too, with steam up. She would tow them through the reef and into the little harbor.

Von Mücke in his pith helmet and white uniform joined the others and snapped orders to the men on the steam pinnace to move. The distance was about two miles, through which the steam pinnace must pick her way, since the water was very shallow in spots and the coral was very sharp. As they moved slowly and carefully the island itself was plainly before them. There was little to see. It was flat and quite undistinguished, covered with palm trees through which could be seen the roofs of the European-style houses of the station attendants and the tall mast of the wireless station. After the landing party had entered the lagoon, von Mücke on the steam launch ordered the helmsman to steer for the wireless aerial. That would be their first objective.

At six-thirty they were on shore. They drew up beside a small white sailing ship. One of the officers asked von Mücke if that, too, was to be destroyed.

"Certainly," said von Mücke. He ordered the lieutenant to have a man prepare it with explosives.

As the landing party pulled into shore, it was met by nine members of the staff of the wireless station. Von Mücke, in his heavily accented English, asked them the location of the station, and since there was no point in refusing to answer, the Englishmen told him. He also asked for the location of the house of the director, and it was pointed out to him. He thanked his respondent and noted that the *Emden* had "plenty of trouble with your wireless and cables."

Once all the men were on shore, von Mücke split the party into three sections. He took one section and assigned one to each of his lieutenants. One section moved to the wireless hut, where an operator was sending messages. A second went to the quarters of the station to round up the personnel. Von Mücke took the second party himself. The third was set to work destroying facilities.

Von Mücke called one of the Englishmen aside and told

him to bring the superintendent of the station. In a few minutes this portly gentleman arrived, agreeable and smiling. He was D. A. G. de H. Farrant, head of the Eastern Extension Telegraph Company's station on the island. He gave his keys to von Mücke, pointed out the various houses in which apparatus was located, and said he had no intention of resisting. He then congratulated von Mücke.

"For what," asked the suspicious first officer of the *Emden.*

"For the Iron Cross," said Farrant. Their wireless had picked up a German news bulletin which announced that the Kaiser had honored all the men of the *Emden.*

Von Mücke hid his pleasure and proceeded to the business at hand. All firearms were to be yielded to the Germans, he said. All Europeans on the island were to assemble in the square in front of the telegraph building.

The Europeans were assembled there and placed under a guard. Two men stood near them, and two others brought one of the machine guns from the cutters. Soon, however, the sun rose high and the square became unpleasant, so the civilians asked if they could shelter in the boat shed, and von Mücke said they could.

One party was sent to destroy the wireless mast. Von Mücke led his men into the offices, where they took axes to the Morse equipment, large demijohns of ink, and pieces of cable. They took all the papers and bundled them up in international code flags and prepared to take them back to the *Emden.* They took all the correspondence from the superintendent's office, hoping to find something that would be of interest to them and would tell the whereabouts of British shipping or other targets for the *Emden.* They destroyed the offices with much breaking of glass and smashing of paneling, then moved to the outbuildings, wrecking the engine room, the four dynamos, and the switchboards and the cables.

The destroyers were very thorough. They even wrecked an inoffensive seismograph that had been placed on the island to record earthquakes and other disturbances.

The third party had begun early on the wireless mast, but it caused them trouble. They drilled holes in the base and inserted dynamite cartridges. The first explosion had no effect at all. The second made the mast sway and list, but did not bring it down. The third blast knocked it down, just after seven-thirty in the morning.

As the men were laying the cartridges, one of the Englishmen came up and asked that the mast be felled away from the tennis courts. It was done.

Then came the problem of finding the cables. All over the island there were signs that referred to the cables, but there was no map that showed their location. At one point close to shore, however, stood a cluster of signs that referred to the cables, and von Mücke calculated, quite rightly, that this was the point where they entered the water. They used the cutters and grappling hooks to bring them up from the water. Although the cables were quite visible in the clear water it took some time to get them on the cutters, and then much longer to cut them with crowbars, axes, and cold chisels. Finally, they cut two of the three cables and dragged the ends out to sea, in opposite directions, so it would be difficult for the English to find them again and make repairs. They did not find the third cable.

One of the lieutenants investigated a galvanized-iron storehouse where cables and other material were stored and blew this up with dynamite, just as von Mücke and his party were finishing with the cables.

There was time for a very little bit of conversation with the English, which was carried out in French, English, Dutch, and Pidgin and very bad German. The English told them about their awards and the *Emden* men told the English about the battle at Penang.

Then from the distance could be heard quick bursts from the *Emden*'s siren, recalling the landing party.

Kapitänleutnant von Mücke assembled his men sharply on the beach. They loaded their guns and the captured documents and newspapers and books aboard the three boats, and set out across the lagoon. Behind them the Englishmen yelled goodbye and snapped pictures with their cameras. The little white schooner, which was to be blown up, was left intact. There was no time to destroy it, as the captain was calling them back to the *Emden* immediately. It was a matter of no consequence. Von Mücke could see from the shore that the *Emden*'s anchor flag was flying at half-mast, which meant she was weighing anchor at that moment. He looked at his watch. It was almost nine-thirty.

15. BEFORE THE BATTLE

WHEN VON MÜCKE took the three boats ashore and they disappeared beyond the harbor entrance, the quiet in the *Emden* became almost unearthly. For the first time the ship must sit outside the harbor and wait, its men, and not the ship itself, occupied in the major task of the moment.

Captain von Müller paced the bridge and kept looking at his watch. He looked at the sky. It was a fair and calm day. He decided that he should waste no time, and sent word to von Guerard that the wireless men should call up the *Buresk* and ask her to come immediately to the island. They would coal before they went on.

No answer came from the *Buresk*. The order was repeated.

Then the island's wireless station broke in to ask what ship this was so nearby that was using wireless.

The *Emden* did not answer.

While this drama was being played in the wireless rooms

of the *Emden* and the station, and the steam pinnace was towing its two cutters toward shore, another series of events was launched on the island.

Very early a Chinese servant had noticed a strange ship lying in the entrance to the lagoon. It was not his place to awaken anyone and tell him, but shortly after six o'clock that morning one of the night wireless men came off duty and began walking back to his quarters. The Chinese stopped him and told him what he had seen.

The wireless operator climbed onto the roof of the wireless building, the tallest on the island, and looked out to the entrance to the harbor. There he saw a warship with four funnels. The station had been exchanging messages with H.M.S. *Minotaur* for several days, and he was sure this was the *Minotaur*, but he hurried off to the superintendent's house to inform him of the arrival.

On the way to the superintendent's house he met the island's doctor, who also climbed the roof and through field glasses noted that the ship was not flying a flag and that her first funnel seemed to be a dummy made of canvas. He came off the roof in time to meet the superintendent, who had dressed hurriedly and was on his way to the office.

Inside, the men at the keys were involved in their strange encounter with the mystery ship. They reported. The superintendent ordered a message to be sent immediately:

"S.O.S. Strange ship in entrance."

This was sent several times with the station's coded signature. Then the message was jammed by transmissions from some nearby point, and the superintendent became certain that he was dealing with the *Emden*. The message was changed.

"S.O.S. *Emden* here."

This message was sent constantly, in spite of the radio interference from offshore, until von Mücke and his men burst into the wireless station and ordered the men away from the keys.

On the *Emden* the captain was annoyed to learn that the station had attempted to send out messages, but was not seriously worried. He was convinced that the nearest ships of any kind were now some 250 miles away and could not pose any danger.

He was assured of it when von Guerard came up to the bridge with a message from an unknown ship which was calling the wireless station. The message was coded, but the wireless operators could estimate from the strength of the transmission that the ship sending was 250 miles away.

The men of the *Emden* now prepared for coaling. The task took longer than usual; this was von Mücke's normal responsibility and he was ashore. Still it was done in good time.

At about seven-thirty in the morning several explosions were heard, coming from the island, and the tall radio mast slowly toppled and fell. All was obviously going as planned.

At nine o'clock Captain von Müller began looking at his watch again. Von Mücke was late; he was to have returned by nine o'clock. As the captain began to show concern about the time, a smoke cloud was reported on the horizon. He first accepted this as the mark of the *Buresk*, which was due around ten o'clock. Although the *Buresk* had not answered the *Emden*'s wireless call she had not specifically been told to respond.

The lookout reported a few moments later that he saw a single funnel and two masts. That was the *Buresk*. Lieutenant von Guerard climbed to the crow's-nest and verified this report.

Yet the smoke cloud was not that of the *Buresk*, or the *Buresk* was inadvertently shielding another ship. The smoke cloud became that of His Majesty's Australian Ship *Sydney*, a heavy armored cruiser. She displaced 5,400 tons, she had a speed of 25.7 knots, and she was armed with eight six-inch guns. This was much more powerful than the *Emden*'s 3,650 tons, 24.5 knots, and ten 4.1-inch guns.

After three months of solid good fortune, the fates of war had turned on the *Emden*. At six-thirty that morning, when Captain von Müller was told that the ship calling the Direction Island wireless station was 250 miles away, actually this ship was the *Sydney*, fifty-five miles away, transmitting under reduced power.

Captain Silver, who was in command of a nearby British convoy, had released the *Sydney* to answer the station's S.O.S., and that transmission was the ship's reply to the station. All the while that Captain von Müller had been waiting impatiently for the landing party, the *Sydney* had been bearing down on the *Emden*.

At nine-fifteen, Captain von Müller became very impatient. He ordered the ship's sirens blown to warn von Mücke that he had exceeded his time limit and to call him in. As the sirens sounded, Captain von Müller saw the approaching ship change course and take on a different appearance. She sported the tall masts of a warship, and at that moment of turning she chose to show her white ensign bearing the Cross of St. George.

Within a few seconds Captain von Müller had ordered the anchor weighed, full steam in all boilers, and the ship cleared for action. There was no time to wait for von Mücke and the landing party. If the *Emden* were caught at anchor she would have no chance.

Just before nine-thirty the frantic activity seen by Kapitän-leutnant von Mücke from the steam pinnace meant that the *Emden*, not more than half prepared, was moving out to battle for her life.

16. END OF THE GRAY SWAN

A T NINE-THIRTY, as the *Emden* steamed slowly forth to engage the enemy ship, the *Sydney* was moving due south. She was then about six miles east of Direction Island. Von Müller took his ship due north in the first move of this game. He was not eager to close with the *Sydney* until his steam was up, and that would not be for another half-hour.

Captain Glossop of the *Sydney* gave von Müller no time to maneuver. As the *Emden* moved out of the entrance to the harbor and ran up the black-and-white battle ensign, Captain Glossop turned the *Sydney* hard to starboard and came straight at her. As the *Emden* moved north, he adjusted his course. At nine-forty he had nearly halved the distance between them.

The *Emden* opened fire at 5,600 yards. The first three salvos of the *Emden*'s guns bracketed the *Sydney*. The fourth salvo struck, and bright-yellow flame began to flash from the center deck.

"Very good, Gaede," Captain von Müller said to his gunnery officer. It was better than good, although the German captain did not know it. One of those shells had struck the fire-control room, and the automatic aiming devices of the *Sydney* were out of action. Her guns must be operated manually from that point on.

That was good luck, but the last bit of it for the *Emden*. Moments later the superiority of the *Sydney* began to count. She was faster and she had steam up. She drew away from the *Emden*, past seven thousand yards, out of her range, but not out of the range of the *Sydney*'s guns. Then she began to cut the German cruiser to pieces.

Ten minutes after the fight began the gunners on the *Sydney* found the range. One of the first hits struck near the bridge, and splinters wounded Gunnery Officer Gaede slightly in the eye. Torpedo Officer Witthoeft was struck in the cheek, and a seaman was also slightly wounded. Captain von Müller was hit but did not even know it at the time.

That was the beginning of the carnage.

Next a shell struck squarely on the wireless room and destroyed it completely. All that remained were a few white-hot plates on the deck.

The *Sydney* drew steadily to a point just outside the *Emden*'s range, and kept that distance, pouring shellfire into the German. A shell struck behind the crow's-nest in the mainmast. Another struck one of the after guns, killing the crew and several of the ammunition carriers.

At ten o'clock there was noticeable slacking in the *Emden*'s fire. Why weren't the men shooting? Captain von Müller asked. The range was too great, Gaede replied. Von Müller swung the ship hard to starboard, then, trying to close with the *Sydney*, but Captain Glossop immediately swung to port in a long curve, maintaining the distance.

The *Emden* now presented her port side to the enemy. One direct hit from the *Sydney* knocked out the *Emden*'s aiming system. Leutnant Zimmermann, in charge of this division in the command turret, was unhurt and picked himself up. All his enlisted men were dead. He moved to the starboard No. 2 gun and began directing fire.

Torpedo Officer Witthoeft asked the captain to move in as close as possible, but it was not possible. The *Emden* had scarcely gotten to full steam, which was still an effective three or four knots slower than the *Sydney*, when a shot penetrated below decks and pierced some of the steam pipes. To the fires that sprouted now was added the heat and misery of steam.

A second hit just after ten o'clock killed every man in the port No. 1 gun crew, and a third hit struck directly into the ready ammunition supply of the port No. 4 gun, blasting crew and gun, including Leutnant von Levetzow, who was in charge of the after guns. In a moment the ship was ablaze aft.

At ten-twenty the *Emden* turned again, still trying to close the distance. The hail of fire continued. The steering system was knocked out, and so was the internal communication system. All that was left now were the men, a handful of guns, and their engines. Orders must be transmitted verbally and in person.

Navigator Gropius went aft to attempt to repair the steering gear. Another shell widened the flames in the stern and cut it off from the rest of the ship. The men retreated as the fire kept following them.

Below decks there was much less damage, since the armor plating gave some protection. Just after ten-twenty, however, a hit on the armored deck pierced through and cut below the water line, sending a stream of sea water and gases from the explosion into the torpedo flat. Leutnant von Hohenzollern, the prince, ordered his men into their smoke bandages—gas masks were not yet in use.

The torpedo tubes were ready, and so were the torpedo-men. They were busy now trying to close the hole that was letting sea water pour onto them. The prince sent a man to find carpenters, but the carpenters were busy elsewhere. He released compressed air from the tanks used to fill the torpedo tubes. This cleared the air, but the leaks could not be stopped. When he had used all the air in the tanks he signaled for more to the port auxiliary engine room. There was no answer. He discovered that the signal system had broken down and that a hit on the auxiliary engine room had knocked it out, too.

At ten-twenty-five the *Emden* managed, by the captain's skillful maneuver, steering with his engines, to close the distance between herself and the *Sydney*, but now most of her guns were silenced, and those that were firing were doing so intermittently. Von Müller asked Gaede why there was not more fire, and the gunnery officer replied that there was not enough ammunition on deck. This represented the carnage of the last half-hour. Most of the ammunition handlers had been killed as they moved across the open decks, and those left found it difficult to move through the debris to serve the guns.

The speaking tube between the bridge and the torpedo room was still open. Through that, Witthoeft ordered his men below to prepare the starboard tube, and the prince did so. Above he could hear the constant clanging of metal and explosions as the *Sydney*'s guns punished the cruiser.

Ten-thirty came, then ten-thirty-five, and ten-forty, but there was no order to fire the torpedo. The *Sydney* had moved away and no longer presented her port side to the *Emden*. At ten-forty, in fact, she fired a torpedo at the *Emden*, but this missed.

The two fighting ships were paralleling one another and criss-crossing paths, as the captains fought for advantages. The *Emden*, most of her guns silent now, could hope to destroy the *Sydney* only with a lucky shot in a magazine or by torpedo, and it was to torpedo the *Sydney* that the *Emden* kept moving, trying always to get close enough but never coming half close enough.

At ten-forty-five the *Sydney*'s starboard guns faced the *Emden*'s port side and blasted furiously. There was a sudden shock, felt throughout the ship, and the foremast began to topple. Down it came, bearing a seaman and Adjutant von Guerard to their deaths.

Just before eleven o'clock another shot from the *Sydney* pierced below the armored deck and the water line. It made a sixteen-inch hole in the torpedo flat, and water began pouring in. The prince and his men abandoned the torpedo flat. First they tried to escape through the armored hatch, but they could not get out. They moved to the torpedo storage hatch and made their way out, fastening the watertight doors behind them to control the leak in that compartment.

When the fire-control mechanism was knocked out and the internal communication system failed, Gunnery Officer Gaede began periodic rounds of all his guns. At one of the port guns he was struck by fragments of an exploding shell and mortally wounded. When the prince stepped up from his torpedo room, he found Gaede lying on the deck near the disabled gun, his uniform red and blood making a little pool around him. He was conscious and thanked the prince for words of condolence, then died.

Ten minutes later, the deck was a shambles. All three funnels were hit; two of them were demolished and the third lay at a crazy angle across the buckled deck. The foremast lay across the port side of the ship, its crow's-nest smashed and the tip underwater.

The surgeons and first-aid parties moved around the decks, searching in the debris for the wounded. There were not enough first-aid men, not enough bandages, not enough morphia to go around.

By eleven o'clock the electrical system in the ship was almost totally destroyed. The ship was being steered from the steering flat. Since the funnels were down the smoke from the boilers could not draw off properly, and the *Emden*'s speed was cut further.

At one of the few remaining guns a boatswain's mate was directing fire, and kept directing it until the end, although his right arm had been shot away and most of his men were wounded.

The end was near, now. A shell carried away the captain's bridge. Luckily he was on the main deck when it struck. The ship was barely navigable. Captain von Müller wished to make one last attempt to get within torpedo range, even though the torpedo room was down. With communications knocked out, orders were passed by a gunner down the engine-room skylight, and only thus was the *Emden* kept moving.

When he learned that the torpedo room was completely useless, and as his guns ceased to fire, and the ship continued to lose speed with her funnels shot away, Captain von Müller decided to run her aground on the coral reefs of North Keeling Island. He reasoned that thus the ship would not fall into the hands of the enemy and that only thus could he save the lives of many of his wounded crew and the men who were stationed below decks. If the ship were to sink, most of them would be lost.

Aboard the *Sydney* Captain Glossop realized that von Müller intended to run his ship aground, and he increased the rate of fire from the *Sydney*'s guns in an attempt to sink the German ship.

At eleven-fifteen the *Emden* ran aground on the south coast of the island. The engines were stopped, then started again, and she was firmly fixed on the reef. Then the fires were put out and the seacocks were opened to let the water in. The captain hoped he had completely wrecked his ship so that she would be of no use to the enemy.

While all this was being done the *Emden* remained under enemy fire. At eleven-twenty the *Sydney* saw that the ship was aground and ceased firing at her. Instead of coming around to pick up survivors, however, she moved off in pursuit of the *Buresk*, which had fled north during the battle, having come up and seen what was in progress.

The captain and his few remaining officers then had an opportunity to begin counting noses and checking on the damage.

Captain von Müller toured the decks, trying to comfort the wounded and dying. As the shooting continued for the few moments after grounding, he gave the ship's company permission to jump overboard if they wished and try to reach the island, a hundred yards away from the reef on which they were fixed. He pulled together a party, led by the prince, to destroy the guns, instruments, and secret books aboard the ship. The locks were removed from the guns, the sights from the measuring instruments. Such treatment was given everything forward and amidships, but the crew could not move aft of the engine-room hatch. The metal there was still red-hot from the fires that had burned. They knew nothing of what had happened to Leutnant Gropius and his men, who had gone back to repair the steering.

The prince tried to go aft from the waist, by creeping between decks. In the laundry they found their Chinese washermen, who had been washing clothes even until the moment they were struck by a shell and crumpled on the deck, the wet garments beside them.

The search party discovered a few wounded men and brought them back to the main deck. They could go no farther aft. The metal was too hot.

The crew assembled above in the forecastle, which was the least damaged part of the ship. Dr. Luther was there; Dr. Schwabe had chosen to try to swim to the island. The forecastle was crowded and smelled of sweat and iodine. The bandages soon ran out and the table linens were secured and torn into strips to serve.

At midday the captain discovered that he had a serious water problem. All the water tanks above the armored deck were destroyed, and the drinking-water compartments were located beneath the torpedo flat, which was filled with sea water. The compartments could not be reached, nor could the pumps be worked to draw the water. Even if the electrical system had been in operation the pumps were damaged by shellfire. The only drinking water available on the ship was that which had been left in the pipes, and this was drawn off. It was scarcely enough to wet the lips of the wounded.

The island represented salvation. Captain von Müller

hoped to find enough coconuts there to serve the wounded at least.

As the sun stood high, the heat was oppressive. All the awnings and sailcloth were stored in compartments that were now underwater. The men were abandoned on the main deck to the sun.

They had no boats. The two cutters and the steam pinnace were in the hands of the landing party at Direction Island. The single remaining boat had been struck by a shell and burned.

A few men had managed to reach the safety of the island by swimming through the surf, and now an attempt was made to make contact with them. A line was floated to the beach by using empty ammunition boxes and matting. But the current sweeping around the island caught the line and carried it away from the surf. Once a line was put into the surf and the men held their breaths in anticipation. It caught on the jagged coral and broke in two. The life-saving gun was found and fired, but it did not carry. Two swimmers took lines around their bodies and tried to swim through the surf, but failed.

The wounded were troubled by the heat and the lack of water and the shortage of medicines. They faced another danger, even more gruesome. As soon as a man was left alone, he was attacked by vicious *Döskoppes*, those great sea birds, who hovered over the helpless and pecked at their eyes. A crew of guards was assembled to kill off these new enemies with cudgels and revolvers.

Captain von Müller counted his dead and wounded and missing, but the action was not yet ended.

All afternoon the survivors sat in the blistering sun. At four o'clock the *Sydney* reappeared, and when she came close enough to be identified the men of the *Emden* could see that she was towing two boats. They were the boats of the *Buresk*.

The *Sydney* had sped away from the helpless *Emden* to capture the *Buresk*, but when they caught the slower merchant ship, Captain Klöpper threw his papers overboard and also opened the seacocks and threw the valves overboard so the ship could not be salvaged.

The boarding party from the *Sydney* spent some time searching the ship and questioning the officers and crew after the capture, and then brought the crew and the boats back to the scene of the battle.

The *Sydney* stopped four thousand yards astern of the *Emden* and raised a signal. The *Emden*'s signal books had been burned or destroyed and no one aboard could read the message, so the captain ordered his signalmen to signal in Morse with flags "no signal book," and one signalman did so; the Englishmen either did not understand it or paid no attention to it. Not a gun on the *Emden* was firing and nearly no one was stirring, but suddenly the *Sydney* again opened fire on the wreck. It was a great tribute to the *Emden* that the *Sydney* would be so much afraid of this helpless enemy, but it was an expensive tribute in terms of lives. Men began to fall, killed and wounded by the shellfire.

Captain von Müller did not know what the enemy intended, so he shouted that his men had permission to jump overboard and swim for shore if they wished. Many did so. The prince seized a plank and jumped over the side, hoping to fight his way to the entrance to the lagoon and the safety of the island. But in a few moments he found half a dozen men had joined him on his plank and it was hopeless to try to navigate. They floated in the water, the gunfire starting new flames aboard the *Emden* above them. Half an hour later the gunfire had ceased and the prince and several of the others saw that they would never make it to the island, so they returned to the ship and were helped aboard by their unwounded comrades.

The captain had neglected, it seemed, to haul down the flag of his wreck, and the English did not know what to make of it, so they had taken no chances. When Captain von Müller hauled down his flag and ran up a white flag of surrender, the firing stopped.

The Australian cruiser still did not send doctors or men to help the wounded and helpless of the *Emden*. They dispatched one of the boats they were towing, which held Leutnant Fikentscher and some of the men of the *Buresk*. The cruiser sped south, this time to Direction Island, where Captain Glossop intended to capture the landing party of the *Emden*.

Now that he possessed a boat, Captain von Müller hoped to communicate with the men on North Keeling Island, but before an attempt could be made to do so, darkness fell, so the men of the *Emden* slept that night uneasily and without food or water.

At dawn the officers and able-bodied men were up again. They hoisted the *Emden*'s flag in an upside-down position, the international distress signal. They had half given up hope that the *Sydney* would return.

The captain again counted heads: Several of the wounded had died during the night, including one horribly burned man whose agonies had been stilled only by heavy inroads into the small supply of morphia.

The men of the *Emden* waited.

They could use the *Buresk*'s boat, but the passage through the surf to the island was treacherous, and if this boat smashed all might be lost. Captain von Müller chose to wait and hope that the *Sydney* would return.

At one o'clock in the afternoon the *Sydney* did reappear, her boats swinging in the davits as she came, showing the Germans that their enemies would take them off the hulk of their ship at last.

First two cutters came across to the dangerous *Emden* and one British officer bargained with the captain: The *Sydney* would only take off the ship's company if von Müller would take personal responsibility for the behavior of the crew.

The captain promised his enemies not to fight them aboard their own ship, and the slow process of shipping off the crew began.

The wounded were removed first, in heavy seas that pounded the *Emden* on her reef and made transportation painful and difficult. The able-bodied came next, and then the officers. The captain was the last man off the ship; he had spent the last hour before departure in unsuccessful attempts to build small fires near the magazines so the ship would blow sky-high and could not be reclaimed by his enemies. Small wonder that Captain Glossop of the *Sydney* had been to such pains to deal carefully with an enemy who normally would be considered helpless.

17. PRISONERS

HE *Emden* was gone, the *Buresk* was scuttled, and as Captain von Müller had feared, the *Markomannia* had run afoul of the enemy too and would cruise the seas no more. The *Pontoporos* lay in Singapore and the Germans from the *Emden* who had gone aboard her were in prison camp. All the men of the *Emden*, then, were accounted for save two groups: those in the landing party and those aboard the *Exford*, which had been sent a thousand miles west to await the *Emden*.

On that ship Lauterbach had a Chinese crew made up from the stoker gang of the *Troilus*. He also had two German petty officers from the *Emden*, one to command the deck and the other the engine room, and seventeen *Emden* seamen. He had the new wireless from the *Chilkana*, and thus although sailing westward as promised, he could pick up the wireless traffic of the area. On November 9 and the day after the air was filled with wireless flashes that referred to the *Emden*. But they were either in code or they were jumbled fragments which told him nothing. Yet when the

131

Emden answered none of the *Exford*'s coded calls, Lauterbach began to sense that something serious had occurred. He suspected that he would not see the *Emden* again.

The *Exford*'s orders were unquestionable: proceed to the middle of the Indian Ocean and wait. So that is what Lauterbach did. He moved to the rendezvous point, a man-made point in a sea of salt water. This rendezvous was simply a set of coordinates on a chart. There was no land nearby, and no port from which they could replenish their dwindling supplies.

A week went by and then another. They circled the rendezvous point, waiting. Their food supply grew short.

The *Exford* remained at her rendezvous point until the ninth day of December. Then and only then Lauterbach decided to take up the second half of Captain von Müller's orders: If the *Emden* did not appear or they ran short of supplies they were to head for a neutral port. The closest neutral port was Padang in Sumatra, seven hundred miles from where the *Exford* sat. Lauterbach had no charts, only his own prodigious knowledge of the Eastern seas to guide him, but they made the run in three days using an atlas of the Indian Ocean as a chart. They arrived off Padang light and could see the houses of the city as the pilot boat put out for the ship when Lauterbach had the pilot flag hoisted.

Just then a ship crept out from between two small islands and approached the *Exford*. She hoisted the British war flag and asked the *Exford* to show her flag. Lauterbach ran up the German naval flag. The other ship, which he recognized as the *Empress of Japan*, a liner converted to an auxiliary cruiser, put a shot across his bow and ordered Lauterbach to heave to. A boat came over bearing the Lauterbach counterpart, a boarding officer and a prize crew. Lauterbach argued that he was in neutral waters. The Englishman said he did not care.

It was too late to sink the *Exford*, although Lauterbach had employed his crew earlier at boring holes in her and sealing them back again so she could be sunk, and given a little time he could have sent her gurgling to the bottom. He barely managed to throw all of his secret papers into the leaded bag and get it over the side. He did manage also to slip the compass from the bridge over the side, leaving his enemies only the compass at the hand steering wheel, which was four points off. He moved that to the bridge, hoping that the prize crew would use it for navigation and would pile the *Exford* onto the rocks. They did.

The officers of the *Empress of Japan* believed that Lauterbach was the commander of the landing party from the *Emden*, and it took some time to convince them that he was not. The captain, Commander Hamilton, treated Lauterbach royally while he was aboard the auxiliary, and with the greatest of respect, because he was an officer from the *Emden*. Eventually, however, Lauterbach was taken to a prison camp in Singapore, along with his men of the *Emden*. Some from the *Pontoporos* and the *Markomannia* were already there. The authorities offered Lauterbach transfer to one of the hotels in Singapore if he would give his parole, his promise not to try to escape. He refused, and he did escape later, to neutral Java and then to the United States, where he began a new set of adventures. He made his way back to Germany and was attached to the staff of Admiral Tirpitz for a time, reported to the admiralty on the exploits of the *Emden*, ran a flotilla of "mystery ships" which were actually raiders, sank several British ships of the same type, was trapped by six British destroyers and escaped in a small boat, commanded the German raider *Moewe*, and went safely through the German naval mutiny.

Captain von Müller and the survivors of the *Emden* were taken in the direction of Colombo aboard the *Sydney*. Several men died in the next two days of injuries sustained in the battle. On November 14 the wounded personnel were transferred to the auxiliary cruiser *Empress of Russia*, which had the room to become a temporary hospital ship.

The *Sydney* and the *Empress of Russia* arrived in Colombo on November 15. That same afternoon the officers and the able-bodied men were shipped aboard various transports, which had been liners. Captain von Müller, Surgeon Luther, Leutnant Fikentscher, and the prince were taken on the *Orvieto*. They were taken in convoy to Aden, to Suez, and finally, aboard the cruiser *Hampshire*, an old friend and an old enemy, to Malta, where they were imprisoned for the remainder of the war.

On the trip to Colombo, Captain von Müller and the others were cheered by one bit of information they received: The reason the *Sydney* had been so long in coming to the assistance of the *Emden* after her surrender was that the landing party of the *Emden* had escaped.

18. MIRACULOUS ESCAPE

WHEN FIRST OFFICER Hellmuth von Mücke of the *Emden*'s landing party saw the *Emden* begin steaming away from him, he was surprised and puzzled. It was true that he had overstayed his time ashore, but no one had expected the task of finding and cutting the submarine cables to take so much time, and since his captain was an understanding if a demanding man, the correct von Mücke anticipated no trouble in explaining his tardiness.

At first, von Mücke believed the *Emden* was moving to meet the *Buresk* to bring her through the shoal water that surrounded the Cocos Islands. He expected to go outside and then catch up with his ship as she slowed to turn and guide the coaler. Then he noticed that she kept increasing her speed until she hit something around sixteen knots, while his launch, laden with two tows, could make but four knots.

Suddenly, as they cleared the reef, he saw the *Emden* run up her battle flags, and saw, then heard, the flashes from her starboard guns as she began firing salvos at an enemy. He did not know what enemy, and he assumed it was a British freighter somewhere out of sight.

Then five spouts in the sea next to the *Emden* showed him that this was not a defenseless merchantman. The *Emden* was engaged in battle. He could not see her opponent from his position, because the island came between the two ships, but he did know that there was no chance of overtaking his ship and that he must wait until she returned. He turned the steam pinnace back to shore.

This time von Mücke knew exactly what he was about. There was no stopping to ask for directions. He sent men to raise the German flag on the staff, and he told the superintendent that the island was now under German martial law. The Englishmen were ordered into one place and their arms were again collected and confiscated. They were warned against trying to communicate with any other island or any ship.

The beach was cleared of civilians and the machine guns were removed to shore and placed so as to sweep the landing area. The sailors began to entrench. Von Mücke was determined to defend the island against a landing party if his ship should be defeated and it should come to that.

When the English superintendent, Mr. Farrant, saw what the Germans were doing, he asked on behalf of his men that the civilians be allowed to move to one of the other islands if it appeared that a fight was going to develop. He did not like the prospects of being targets without being able to fight back. Von Mücke assented to this course, and cordiality was maintained.

Von Mücke took two of his signalmen and climbed to the top of the wireless office, the highest building on the island. There he watched, as well as he could, the fight between the two cruisers. He saw the *Emden* under fire, and the *Sydney*'s shells falling around her, and commented, without knowing of the destruction of the *Sydney*'s rangefinder, on the poor shooting of the enemy. Then the gun aimers found the range, and before von Mücke's anguished eyes the *Emden* began to spout smoke and flame. He saw the forward funnel shot away, the shell that began the huge blaze aft that cost the life of Navigator Gropius.

He saw the quick turn to starboard and the fall of the foremast, and knew that it cost the life of some officer, but he did not know it was young von Guerard who died.

The ships moved northward, away from the island, and soon were out of sight, but von Mücke, a trained naval officer, need see no more than he had. He knew that the *Emden* had met a superior enemy armed with much heavier guns, that she was taking terrible punishment without being able to return very much, and that unless she could fire a torpedo that would stop or sink the enemy, her chances of survival were slim. He also could see that the other ship was faster than the *Emden*, and he knew how little was the chance that his captain would ever be able to fire that torpedo.

So von Mücke knew that he was now commander of a detachment of the Imperial German Navy and he alone must decide what use should be made of his troops. Even if the *Emden* escaped from the Englishman, and he now knew the other ship to be either the *Sydney* or the *Melbourne*, the German cruiser would be forced to run for some neutral port in hopes of making repairs and escaping again. She would never come back to Direction Island.

Whatever the outcome of the battle, von Mücke knew, he could expect a British warship to come to the island very shortly. If the enemy ship out there to the north was sunk, which seemed most unlikely, still there would be another cruiser along within a few hours at the most. Britain would not stand by and allow her wireless station to go unmourned or allow her cable system to remain out of commission forever. The very success of his shore mission had guaranteed his imminent discovery.

Von Mücke saw two courses, but they were not those a lesser man might have seen. First was to stay and fight, inflict as much damage on the enemy as possible, and then either die or surrender when the ammunition ran out. He did not consider surrendering without a fight. His second course was to take the little schooner that lay in the harbor and escape.

Von Mücke said nothing to his men. He indicated the little schooner, the *Ayesha*, and expressed some interest in going aboard her. Her name, he discovered, was given to honor the favorite wife of Mohammed. Did she have ammunition or guns aboard? Ostensibly to discover this for himself he boarded the steam pinnace and went out to the schooner to see, really, if she was seaworthy.

The captain and one seaman were aboard. Von Mücke began asking casual questions and looking about, and he satisfied himself that she was seaworthy. Then he returned to shore and issued his orders. They would board the *Ayesha* and escape.

Late in the afternoon, as the *Sydney* was pulling up to the hulk of the *Emden*, the *Ayesha* was ready, and the Germans got into their cutters and the pinnace and made for the schooner, giving three cheers, *"Hoch, hoch, hoch,"* as they left. The English responded with hurrays, and then began snapping pictures of the departing enemy.

The Germans boarded the *Ayesha* and assembled aft. Von Mücke made a short speech; the German battle ensign was broken out on the aftermast and saluted with three cheers. The steam pinnace took a line from the bow of the schooner and towed her out of the lagoon. Darkness was falling as she moved outside the reef and her sails caught the light breeze. Had the *Sydney* been about her business, and had she pulled into Direction Island harbor that night, she might have captured the landing crew of the *Emden* even then, for laden with the pinnace and the cutters the *Ayesha* made much less than her eight knots. First Officer, now Captain, von Mücke climbed into the top of the foremast himself and conned his little ship through the reefs and shoals, for he had not a single chart and did not know the waters. He had the boatswain's whistle about his neck on a chain and tooted to the helmsman to steer port or starboard. It soon grew so dark that he could not see from the foremast, so he climbed down into the chains on the port side of the ship, and there, next to the water, gave his orders.

The *Sydney,* which drew up in victorious leisure beside the island, decided that the next morning would be quite enough time to send boats into shore and capture the landing crew of the *Emden.* And so the long quiet night passed, the last few men of the *Emden* inching their way out to sea and to freedom.

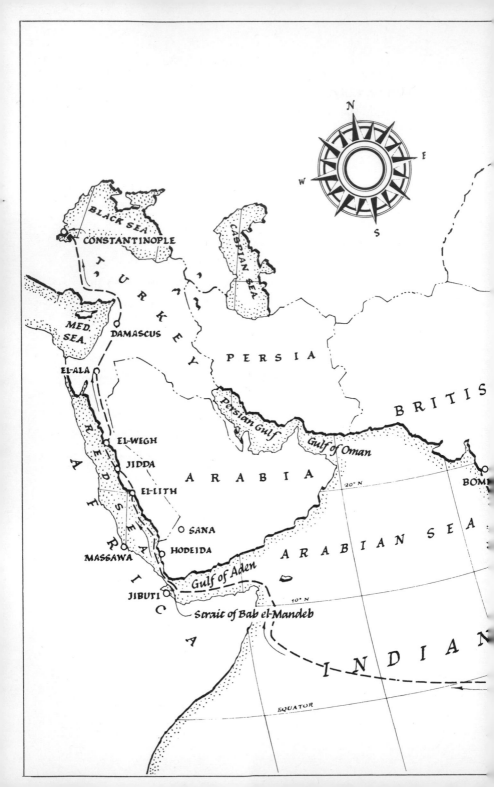

From Cocos Keeling to Constantinople

Scale of Statute Miles

0   200   400   600   800   1,000

Course of von Mücke and his men

CHINA

TIBET

INDIA

BURMA

FRENCH INDOCHINA

SIAM

SOUTH CHINA SEA

BORNEO

CALCUTTA

RANGOON

Gulf of Siam

Andaman Sea

MALAY STATES

SINGAPORE

BAY OF BENGAL

CEYLON

SUMATRA

Java Sea

BATAVIA

PADANG

MADRAS

OCEAN

EQUATOR

JAVA

10° S

COCOS KEELING IS.

20° N

10° N

19. THE AYESHA

EFORE DAWN the *Ayesha* was out of sight of land, away from the many small islands of the Cocos group and safe in deep water where the long swell of the Indian Ocean helped the breeze fill her sails.

That night the men made do about the little ship, sleeping where they might. The next day Captain von Mücke set about, in his thorough navy way, to create order and discipline on his ship. Some of the men had told Englishmen on Direction Island that von Mücke was a "regular Prussian." They were referring to his behavior, not to his Saxon parentage, obviously. But disciplinarian that he was, von Mücke proved before and was to prove again that he would never ask a man to do something he would not do himself; and he led his men, he did not drive them, into every adventure.

On the morning of November 10, the *Ayesha* was sailing nicely in a fresh breeze and von Mücke took his chance to look around him. His ship, his first command, was ninety feet long and twenty-five feet wide and had a burden of ninety-seven tons.

She was a copra ship, by and large, although at the time she was empty and in ballast, carrying iron pigs in the hold. She was painted white, with a figure of her Mohammedan namesake below the long bowsprit, and had three tall masts made from double spars lashed together. The foremast was square-rigged, but the mainmast and mizzenmast were rigged for fore-and-aft sails. This gave her the double advantage of navigability on the high seas and in the coastal waters where the wind is changeable.

She was intended for a five-man crew and was found for that purpose. Her two small boats, her cabins, her galley were all built for the small crew. This created the most difficult problem with which the men of the *Emden* had to deal on the *Ayesha,* since there were ten times as many of them as the ship could comfortably accommodate. The forecastle of the *Ayesha,* for example, could house only six men at the most.

The sleeping problem was solved by assigning most of the men berths in the hold. They had brought with them a few blankets and mattresses. But the men bedded down on the spare sails in the hold, with the iron ballast for mattresses. As time went on they solved the sleeping problem for themselves by making hammocks from ropes and sailcloth.

Below deck were two small cabins, which the Germans used to store the provisions they had taken from the island. Far aft was another cabin, which was called the chart room, where the petty officers were quartered. Captain von Mücke lived in the deckhouse in a small cabin, and his two lieutenants shared another the same size, and a third, still smaller cabin was fitted up as an officers' mess, smoking, and wine room, also to be used by the officer on watch as his watchroom.

Immediate attention had to be paid to the problem of the galley, for it was totally unfit to serve fifty men. Several pigs of iron ballast were brought up from the hold and laid out to form a fireproof stove. Pieces of sheet iron and tin were taken from the interior of the ship and wrapped around this to hold it together and create a flat surface. It was more an open fireplace than a stove. The men cooked by holding the pots over the flames on rods.

Captain von Mücke selected a cook and several assistants and gave them the keys to the storerooms. They had plenty of tinned foods and sacks of rice, so they would not go hungry.

The water problem was more serious. The 150 gallons he had brought from the island was not drinking water but contaminated fresh water used by the islanders only for their machinery. A few days out, von Mücke discovered that their fresh water supply was gone. He had several cases of bottled soda water on board, but did not wish to use that save in an emergency, particularly if they had to abandon the *Ayesha* and go back into the cutters. But on this first day von Mücke did not worry about water. He had the water, he thought, safe in four iron tanks. He was more concerned about sea water coming in than fresh water going out. Captain Partridge had mentioned to him that the *Ayesha*'s bottom should be checked for signs of rot, and von Mücke went below to investigate. Sure enough, when he plunged his knife into her planking it came out red and covered with long rotten fibers. She was pulpy and leaky both, and soon the water began to rise in her. He checked the pump, but it would not work, and he set men to dismantling it. The leather packing was dried and rotten, so it was replaced with rags soaked in oil and then worked serviceably.

On the fourth day out from Direction Island they discovered the water problem, but it bothered them only for a few hours. The tanks were cleaned out and a sail was spread on deck, horizontally across the main hatch with a hole in the middle. Below the hole in the hold stood a five-gallon petroleum can. That afternoon the tropical rain came with its usual quick ferocity. Men went below and formed a chain gang, passing the petroleum cans as they filled, dumping them into the tanks, and returning them beneath the sail for refill. The roof of the deckhouse was also made into a rain catcher by fastening molding around the sides and making gutters that ran into petroleum cans. The men of the *Ayesha* did not suffer for lack of drinking water.

The men had come aboard in their summer white uniforms and with only such extra clothing as they had been able to beg from the men of Direction Island. In a few days their clothes were in tatters; to save what remained the men worked the ship in their underwear and sometimes in no clothes at all.

The crew shared one comb and one razor. The comb was used daily by nearly everyone, the razor by very few, and it soon grew rusty and hardly usable at all. A light watch was kept at night, but most of the men slept nights and arose at six o'clock in the morning to begin the day's work of keeping the ship fit and clean.

They doused the decks in salt water by hauling pails up over the side in the traditional manner of sailing-ship sailors. One watch went to work on the pumps, pulling out the water that had leaked into the hold overnight. There was tea in the morning for breakfast, with rice, and gooseberry wine with lunch and coffee in the evening, again with rice.

In the evenings they sang old German songs, sentimental

and sad ones for the most part, but happy ones, too. There was a marked absence of military songs on these occasions. The war seemed far off as they lay on the deck of the silent schooner, listening to the sounds of the sea and watching the moon and the stars that are so much brighter in the Southern skies than in the North.

One day the men of the *Ayesha* were becalmed when they saw a smoke cloud on the horizon. The steamer traveled along the horizon for several hours before disappearing, giving the crew of the sailing ship much anxiety, for they did not know whether it would be friend or foe, and they were nearly defenseless on their tiny sailing vessel.

The matter of defense was all in how one looked at it. As far as defense against civilians and savages was concerned, the *Ayesha* was strong. Captain von Mücke had mounted the four machine guns on deck and had cut holes through the solid rail of the main deck so the guns could be trained at a ninety-degree angle of coverage. Against unarmed men or men armed only with rifles this was a formidable show of force. Against even a patrol boat with a single small cannon it was no force at all. Von Mücke knew this and knew that his one chance of reaching a neutral port and safety was to avoid all shipping at all costs. His greatest fear was a Japanese or English patrol boat, because this was the type of vessel that was most likely to take an interest in the schooner.

At ten o'clock in the morning on November 23, when the *Ayesha* had been at sea for two weeks, land came into sight. Von Mücke had been navigating with a large map of the Eastern Hemisphere, which represented the eight hundred miles from the Cocos Islands to Sumatra as about the breadth of a hand. He was not quite certain if he had even managed to hit Sumatra, or the Dutch East Indies for that matter. One tiny island gave place to the next as the *Ayesha* threaded her way through the shallow water. At four o'clock in the afternoon some of those who were more familiar with the South Seas than von Mücke realized where they were and said they were just outside Seaflower Channel, about eighty miles from Padang.

The breeze that night and the next morning was blowing offshore, and it was a light breeze. The *Ayesha* made practically no progress all day long, although the men could plainly see the mountains and forests of Sumatra. The wind slackened several times almost to dead calm, the heat grew oppressive, and finally they were forced to bring up a spare sail and spread it above the deck as an awning. That night they saw Padang light, but they also saw that they were passing it at a great distance. The breeze continued offshore and light, there was no chance to tack, and by morning they discovered that they were five miles farther from Sumatra than they had been on the night before.

On November 25, finally, the wind came up and began to blow ashore for a change. In the distance the crew of the *Ayesha* could see steamers moving in and out of the harbor at Padang. One of them seemed to be lying very still, and then suddenly, belching great black clouds of smoke, she headed straight for the sailing vessel at high speed. Captain von Müller, familiar with ways of small ships, would have spotted her immediately as a patrol boat from her smoke, but the crew of the *Ayesha* were unsure until she came very close, and then they could, with relief, see that she bore the flag of the Netherlands at her masthead.

20. PADANG

ON NOVEMBER 27 the *Ayesha* finally came within Dutch territorial waters, and she ran up her German war ensign when Captain von Mücke was certain she was inside the three-mile limit.

After the *Ayesha* had sent about a sixth of her anchor chain out to reach the bottom of the harbor, and all was made secure, von Mücke sent Leutnant Schmidt ashore to report their arrival to the Dutch port authorities officially and to pay a call on the German consul and request that he come to the ship. Other than port officials and government officials, no one was to be allowed on board the *Ayesha* and no one was to be allowed off except on official business.

Within an hour the identity of the newcomer was known all over the harbor, and soon the boats of three German ships were in the water, bringing greetings, gifts, and newspapers from home to the men of the *Ayesha,* who had not seen a German newspaper since July. The newspapers were six weeks old, but what did that matter? For the first time the crew felt they had some contact with the war in Europe.

None of the Germans from these other ships came aboard the *Ayesha,* but they threw their gifts up to the deck. It would have been a breach of international law for them to have gone any further in making contact in a neutral port.

Captain von Mücke was having enough trouble with the law and the Dutch interpretation of it as matters already stood, without courting trouble. Goaded by the British representatives in Padang, the Dutch authorities first took the position that the *Ayesha* was a prize of war and that she could not be sailed out of the harbor.

Captain von Mücke replied that the *Ayesha* was a German warship and any affront to her was an affront to the Kaiser and the Imperial German government. He said he would account only to his superiors in the navy for his right to command the *Ayesha.* He demanded permission to take on water, provisions, charts, and equipment. The German consul began making arrangements for the purchase and shipment of the supplies to the harbor. The legal complications might take some time but the supplies must be made available in any case.

As they argued the provisions began to come alongside, and the harbormaster was mute when asked if they might be loaded. His lack of response was taken to be assent and the tins of food and other supplies came aboard, along with ten live pigs who milled around on the deck near the anchor housing.

The Dutch officers finally gave them permission to leave the harbor. They were nearly as much trouble to the men of the *Ayesha* as their pork on the hoof. The pigs held up matters for some time because they refused to move from the foredeck and allow the crewmen to heave in the anchor.

21. END OF THE AYESHA

As the *Ayesha*'s crew unfurled her topsails and the schooner began to move out of the harbor, Kapitän-leutnant von Mücke of the Imperial German Navy led the fifty men in singing the Fatherland song: *Es braust ein Ruf wie Donnerall"* ("There roars a call, a thunderous sound") and in martial vigor the most unlikely ship of His Majesty's Navy passed out to sea.

The *Ayesha* sailed and drifted in the calm for three weeks. Her rolling in the calm was matched by her pitching in rough weather. The pigs, in particular, were discomfited. Since they had taken so great a liking to the capstan and the bows, von Mücke had a pigpen constructed around them. As the weather grew rough he had to send men up forward to nail slats to the deck so the poor creatures were not forever sliding back and forth.

On December 14, the *Ayesha* was sailing in an area where she hoped to meet a German ship when a ship suddenly loomed ahead through the thick rain and fog of the day. The *Ayesha* had been sailing back and forth, east and west,

150

for some days, searching. Now, sailing west, they saw that the other ship was sailing east, which meant that she was bound on some mission other than making way between two ports. In this part of the Indian Ocean ships did not sail east and west to make port. From the moment of sighting, von Mücke sensed that this was his countryman. The problem was not to be careful and check her, but to attract her attention. Even at four thousand yards there was grave danger that the merchantman might miss her in this soupy weather, and the chance of escape from the Indian Ocean would be gone. Von Mücke had no illusions about his hopes of sailing the *Ayesha* across the Indian Ocean, through the Red Sea, the Mediterranean, under the guns of Gibraltar, and then to Germany. His hope from Padang had been to encounter a German ship and transfer his crew to that vessel, taking charge of it in the name of the Imperial Navy. Here was his chance. The ship was the German freighter *Choising*.

The *Ayesha* began signaling to the *Choising* and for once put on all the sail the little ship would carry, desperately hoping to close with her and show herself before the other passed in the fog. The signalman produced the signaling pistol and they fired their precious supply of red and white fireballs, a half-dozen shots.

At last these attracted the attention of someone on the *Choising*'s bridge, and the merchant ship turned and headed back toward the schooner. Immediately the *Ayesha* ran up flags and streamers which identified her as a German warship. The *Choising* hoisted her German ensign, too. Most of the fifty men aboard the *Ayesha* clambered into the shrouds, cheering and shouting.

Von Mücke took charge at once. He saw that the seas were too rough to board the *Choising* safely, so he signaled the merchant ship to follow him and turned south, where he expected to find better weather.

Contrarily, the weather turned worse instead of better. The next day the *Ayesha* was taking heavy seas, but she rode them well and her rigging seemed to withstand the tortures of the storm. The *Choising*'s captain became very nervous and signaled that he must get out of this weather and the shoal water into which they were heading. A new rendezvous was arranged and the *Ayesha* was again left alone.

The night of December 15 was the worst the men of the *Ayesha* spent aboard their little ship. The storm was so severe that they could see nothing, and the tossing of their schooner so severe that they were wet and miserable and afraid all night long. They were being blown onto some small islands of the East Indies chain; both current and wind were carrying them toward the reefs, and so it was necessary to keep canvas on the ship to stand away from the land. Closely reefed as the sails were, they were not strong enough to stand the storm. First the foresail and the staysail tore away. The foresail was scarcely gone when the fore staysail went, too. It was impossible to rig new canvas, and so the ship sailed with her after sails alone, and with hope that these would keep her off the beach.

They did. The wind died down, and the next morning the crew bent new sails and headed toward the second rendezvous, arriving at nine o'clock in the morning, in the bright sunshine, with the welcome sight of the *Choising* steaming down on them from the distance.

Von Mücke signaled the *Choising* to take the sailing ship into tow in the calm and to make for the lee of one of the small islands nearby. There the men of the *Emden* would leave their little vessel.

In the interim, as the sailing ship was under tow, the navy men began to unrig their ship. All the arms were brought on deck, all the provisions were brought up to be taken along. The figurehead was taken down and the wheel was taken off its post; both would be carried along by the men of the *Emden* as souvenirs of their voyage and given to the navy in Berlin.

In the lee of the tiny island the job of destruction was begun. The *Ayesha*'s shrouds were cut through and holes were bored in the hull. At four o'clock in the afternoon the transfer was completed and the *Choising* started her engines, moving away, planning to leave the sailing ship. But the *Ayesha* followed, and a few moments later, as if angered by her treatment, she fouled the ship of those who had betrayed her, carrying away much of the gangway ladder. The *Choising* was stopped then, and von Mücke and his men watched the little schooner sink. It took her fifty-eight minutes to go down, her decks slowly sinking below the water, the bow rising, and falling and rising again. Finally the pigs of iron below must have shifted forward, because she turned her bowsprit under and went down like a porpoise diving, the cheers of her last crew ringing above her grave.

22. DESTINATION: ARABIA

CAPTAIN MINKIEWITZ of the *Choising* was a loyal German officer and a forbearing man; even so it was difficult for him to place himself under the orders of the brusque Captain von Mücke who now took charge of the *Choising* without apology. Yet Captain Minkiewitz behaved nobly from the beginning.

Von Mücke wasted no time in making preparations to move in secrecy and as swiftly as the seven-and-a-half-knot speed of the *Choising* would allow. She did not even make that speed most of the time, because she was carrying an inferior grade of coal. At one time, the *Choising* had been designated as coaler for the *Emden;* this was one reason that Captain Minkiewitz was so quick to respond to von Mücke's call. She was one of those ships for which the *Emden* had searched at the beginning of her voyage and had not found. In the *Choising*'s case there was no mystery about it: while waiting for the *Emden* her cargo of Australian and Indian coal had been fired by spontaneous combustion and she had left the rendezvous to put out her fires.

The fires had been extinguished, and now the survivors of the *Emden* made their beds in the coal storage. This time they had mattresses and plenty of blankets, however, and the quarters were far more comfortable than those they had just left atop the *Ayesha*'s pig iron. The new captain and his officers took over the bridge and the choice accommodations, and the captain of the *Choising* yielded, in effect, his command.

The next problem, which must be decided immediately, was a course. Where did the men of the *Emden* propose to go?

Von Mücke planned to make his way home to Germany to fight again. (He never considered anything less than fighting again.) This presented some serious problems. Should he try to provision the ship somewhere and steam around the Cape of Good Hope, and then make his way through the English Channel and to the North Sea? All the way he would be in danger of running afoul of British warships.

A newspaper he found aboard the *Choising* gave von Mücke hope that another course would be possible. He saw a report of a battle between Turkish and British troops at Sheikh Said, near Perim, an island in the Strait of Bab el-Mandeb. This was a definite indication that Turkey was in the war, although he had not seen or heard of any declaration. Searching, then, among the old newspapers on the *Choising,* von Mücke found the declaration of war of November 5, which followed the raid on the Russian Black Sea coast by Turkish warships and the German cruisers *Goeben* and *Breslau,* masked as Turkish vessels. He also learned that nine days later the sultan had declared a holy war on the English, which gave von Mücke hope that he would find friendly Arabs in the Arabian Peninsula. So, he evolved a plan in a very few hours. The *Choising* would take the men of the *Emden* to the Arabian Peninsula and they would disembark to make their way overland to Turkey and fight again for the Kaiser.

Now, an end in mind, Captain von Mücke looked over his new command. She was a German Lloyd steamer, and like all of that line, she wore the company uniform: black hull, white bulwarks, and ocher trim. This must be remedied, and it was. She was painted over, a single drab color. Then she looked like a Dutchman, but this was unsatisfactory, because the British were bound to take an inordinate interest in a neutral ship. Looking over the shipping lists in Captain Minkiewitz's cabin, von Mücke discovered that a 1,700-ton vessel named the *Shenir* had recently been transferred from British to Italian registry. Since the Italians were still vacillating about their entry into the war (and would until late 1915), von Mücke chose to masquerade the *Choising* as an Italian ship, with the thought that the British would not harry an Italian. The *Shenir* was exactly the size of the *Choising,* so on the stern of the Lloyd steamer was painted the wording: "*Shenir,* Genoa." All that was needful, von Mücke hoped, was that the Chinese crew of the *Choising* be kept out of sight when British ships were in the vicinity.

There was one other need, an Italian flag. There was none aboard the *Choising,* so one was manufactured. A green window curtain was sewed to a strip of red cloth and a strip of white cloth, and a volunteer artist from among the men of the *Emden* set about painting the coat of arms of the Italian kingdom on the white strip. The green window curtain was not the right color, so it had to be stripped off. Then the artist mixed blue and yellow paint to obtain the correct shade and dipped the curtain into it. When it was dry he sewed the curtain back onto the red and white and had a very presentable Italian flag, as long as it did not rain.

While the artist worked over the flag, Captain von Mücke set a course westward to cross the Indian Ocean slightly south of its center, avoiding the steamer lanes always and keeping out of the typhoon region. There was only one real task for the men of the *Emden,* and that was to keep sharp lookout all around the horizon. Discovery in their case meant instant capture, and so they crept through the Indian Ocean hoping they would be unseen.

23. THE LANDING

THE VOYAGE across the Indian Ocean was totally without incident. The *Choising* made the trip in twenty-two days, an excellent time considering the slowness of the ship and the out-of-the way route she followed. They were not stopped by any steamers and had no difficulties. There was no shortage of food or drink or any other trouble. Christmas was celebrated as a religious holiday, but on New Year's Eve they broke out the beer and wine and finished up the entire supply on the ship. Then all was quiet until they arrived at the Strait of Bab el-Mandeb, the southern gateway to the Red Sea, on January 7, 1915.

They approached the strait on the African side, without lights. Von Mücke wanted to take no chance of detection, so the lights were extinguished, and his officers and petty officers patrolled the ship to be sure the Chinese crew members did not show a light in carelessness.

Von Mücke ordered the helmsman to steer very close to the African shore, hoping to be hidden there against the dark horizon. The revolving light on Perim Island nearly undid him, for regularly its beam fell on the ship like a searchlight. He could see two English warships lying just off the island, signaling to one another in Morse with their lights.

The *Choising* inched past, von Mücke certain that they must be discovered at any moment. The inching took half an hour, and astonishingly to von Mücke they were not seen. Outside the perimeter of the light they were still in danger for another hour, but the seas blew up and ran high, which helped protect them and helped keep the minds of others on seamanship.

All night long the men of the *Emden* kept worried lookout, even when outside the straits. The next day they watched the horizon anxiously, even when they were in the broad Red Sea. They did their best, again, to avoid detection by staying well away from the steamer lanes.

Captain von Mücke decided to land Kapitänleutnant von Mücke and the fighting men of the *Emden* near Hodeida and try to reach that Arab city. The best information he possessed, which came from an old guidebook, told him that Hodeida was a large commercial city and that a dozen years earlier, when the book was published, the Hejaz railway was being built to connect Hodeida with a number of other points in Arabia. So, as far as von Mücke knew, there was a railroad, and it should lead him eventually to Constantinople and thus to Berlin. He did not put aside the contingency that the railroad might not be operating, however. If there was no road, the side trip was still valuable, for at Hodeida they could find charts of the Red Sea and would learn what was happening in the war.

The four boats were ready to go over the side, and the men of the *Emden* were ready to move. Dr. Lang, the ship's physician on the *Choising,* was persuaded to accompany the men of the *Emden,* so now they had their own doctor and some medicines.

As they came near to the area where they expected to find Hodeida, von Mücke saw from the bridge that the town was brightly lighted.

At least the port was. This gave him hope that the railroad would be running and that in two weeks they would be on the North Sea, assigned to another powerful German warship.

As they neared the lights, these began to move, to change position relative to the shore. Port lights do not do that, so von Mücke took alarm. The engines of the *Choising* were stopped and soundings were made. He calculated that they were in twenty fathoms of water and that the port must be several thousand yards away, but the lights were very close. Abruptly he had the feeling that he had best get away from those lights, so he took the ship sixteen miles north, before the boats were put into the water.

The order was given for the men to get into the boats, and this time it was not countermanded. When the men of the *Emden* were aboard, the fourteen-foot boats were heavily laden. Three of them were rigged in German fashion, and a fourth was rigged as a sampan, which would certainly cause some raised eyebrows if sighted by knowledgeable seagoing men along the coast.

Von Mücke gave some last instructions from the bridge. The captain of the *Choising* was handed his written orders, to spend the next two days in the vicinity of a given point outside the steamship routes, and on the next few nights to return each night to the point of departure and wait. If the men did not return after a week he was to proceed to Massawa, a port in Italian Somaliland.

Von Mücke was operating totally in the dark. He did not know who was in control of Hodeida or the area into which he was piercing. If his enemies were in control he intended to hide in the desert during the daylight hours and make his way back to the sea at night.

He had considered every eventuality, it seemed. If there was danger to the *Choising* the shore party would send rocket signals, and these would mean the captain of the ship was to break off and proceed immediately to Massawa. By this von Mücke meant unusual danger. There was danger to the ship and its crew every moment they spent in these waters that were dominated by the French and English.

The crews of the four boats raised their sails and the men began to bail. All the boats leaked, since they had not been in the water for a long time. That is how the night was spent, sailing and bailing, until the sun popped up over the flat horizon and the day's heat began. Early in the morning, before the shimmering heat haze set in, von Mücke could see for a long distance, and he saw that the "port" he had observed the night before was actually a French heavy cruiser, the *Desaix,* anchored beside the Italian ship *Juliana.*

As the light came up, Kapitänleutnant von Mücke brought his boats to anchor and the rigging was stripped down. It would never do to have questions asked about the Chinese rig on one of them. It was best to appear as fishermen, and they could do this with bare masts showing, but hardly otherwise. They could not remain long, however, because they would be seen and undoubtedly investigated by that cruiser. So they pulled for shore.

Near the shoreline they encountered an Arab fishing boat whose occupant was all smiles at seeing so many men in small boats. He grinned and gesticulated happily, and spoke to them in his native tongue. Von Mücke and the others tried a succession of languages on him, but the fisherman understood nothing. He seemed to understand the words *français* and *Franzose,* and by conversing loudly and in vigorous sign language plus German, von Mücke was able to gather that indeed the French did occupy Hodeida, thank you very much.

His heart fell, and he was only slightly consoled when the four boats all managed to make the far side of the surf without swamping or capsizing.

The shore was long and sloping. They were through the surf and on the beach, and yet were half a mile from land. They made rafts of the oars and masts and some lifeboats and floated their guns and supplies in to shore.

On the shore they encountered two Arabs, who ran away from the landing party in spite of von Mücke's gestures of friendship. Then up came an armed man riding a camel. He was dressed in a red-and-blue uniform, with a headcloth of the Arab style. Von Mücke did not know whether he was a French soldier or of what army, but since the man sat on his camel, pointing a cocked gun in their general direction, he gathered that here was a soldier. He approached the man on the camel alone and without guns, starting from the point about six hundred yards away from the group where the soldier had stopped his camel.

Von Mücke took a few steps forward. The soldier raised his gun. Von Mücke stopped. The soldier lowered his gun. Von Mücke started forward, hopefully. The soldier raised his gun. Von Mücke stopped, and the gun went down; he moved again, and the gun went up. This ballet continued until he reached a point fifty yards from the soldier, where the gun stayed up when he stopped. He went no farther, but began to try to make conversation, an effort as futile as talking with his fisherman acquaintance back in the boat.

After von Mücke had exhausted his knowledge of communication without language, and without the slightest effect, the soldier indicated by a gesture that the party was to remain where it was, and wheeled off.

In the distance von Mücke could see the white houses of Hodeida. What was to be done now?

Kapitänleutnant von Mücke proposed to take his men to hide in the dunes around them and then to send an officer into Hodeida at night to seek information. If the French were truly there, then the next night they would return to the sea and reembark on the *Choising*, making an alternate plan when they could.

He was making ready for a brief march when from behind the sandhills came a swarm of Bedouins, around a hundred strong, all armed with rifles. They formed a skirmish line and dropped down to the ground. The Germans picked up their guns and made ready for a fight. They dropped to the ground, and formed themselves into a loose semicircle, facing the land. Von Mücke waited for the first shot.

Instead of a shot, from the hills came a dozen men, unarmed, who were making gestures that seemed to be peaceful and seemed to call for a meeting. Von Mücke put down his sword and pistol and walked to meet them. Then began the parley.

Von Mücke spoke in German, French, and English. The Bedouins spoke in gibberish as far as he was concerned. He had his German flag brought to the meeting and explained what it was. The Bedouins looked at it, fingered it and nodded understandingly. They had not the slightest idea what it might be.

He pointed to the French cruiser offshore and shook his fist, shouting "boom, boom, boom" as he did so. The Bedouins grinned at his lively act.

The Bedouin leaders then had their turn. One held his head with his hand, as though he had a terrible ache in both temples, and wagged his head violently from side to side to relieve the pain. Another, who the Germans thought might be suffering from neuralgia, passed two fingers up and down his face. A third rubbed his two extended forefingers together.

This last sign was quite clear to von Mücke. He was certain that it meant enemies, because the rubbing was friction. And he pointed to the rubbing and said it was not true. The Arabs knew he did not understand, then, because all these signs were signs of friendship, and this tall, blond, stupid man was telling them they were not friends but enemies.

Von Mücke's officers had come forward by this time, trying to lend a hand. Leutnant Wellman spoke to the Arabs in Malay. It was as effective as von Mücke's German. In despair, Leutnant Schmidt reached into his pocket and pulled forth a gold piece. He pointed to the head of the Kaiser on it.

"Aleman! Aleman!" shouted the Bedouins in instant comprehension, fingering the gold piece.

Immediately the beach became a shambles. The Arabs stacked their guns and then came flying down the dunes, their white and gray and black robes trailing behind them and the sand flying in spurts from beneath their feet. They embraced the Germans, danced wildly around them, shouted words that must mean friendship, and insisted on carrying the Germans' guns and gear. First, however, they insisted on looking into it. The sailors gave them some soap, which sent their new friends into ecstasy, and soon the bundles were shouldered and a certain amount of order was restored to the gathering.

They moved towards Hodeida. The desert seemed grim and empty, but as they came by heads began popping up and soon another hundred armed men and boys joined the procession.

If the French were in possession of Hodeida, they would certainly know that something was coming.

But the French were not in possession. Hodeida was safely in Turkish hands, courtesy of the Arabs. Half an hour after they began, before they reached the city, still another two hundred Bedouins appeared, guns at the ready, wanting to find out what all the shouting was about. They, too, joined the throng when they learned about the marvelous gold piece.

Before they reached Hodeida, the German landing party had gathered a crowd of about eight hundred Arabs about them, all armed, all shooting their guns into the air enthusiastically, and most of them dancing about the desert as they went.

An armed party of Turkish soldiers appeared well before they came to the city, cautiously scouting this unknown menace. The Bedouins were able to make themselves understood above the shouting, and the Turks came down from the heights on which they sat, gingerly riding in among the mob. One of the Turkish officers spoke German. After a few words he turned in his saddle and barked a stream of Turkish at a soldier, who dashed off on his horse.

What was that all about, von Mücke wanted to know.

The soldier was going back to the garrison, the officer said. The entire force had been alerted and the artillery was being brought out to repel this landing. The word had come that a large force of British or French had made its way ashore and the entire garrison was on its way to fight.

Now, as they approached the city, von Mücke ordered his men into a military unit, the German war flags flying and their guns carried in military fashion. They stepped smartly as they came into the city, surrounded by Turkish troops and the undisciplined Arabs, and they sang one German marching song after another to keep cadence. From the windows and the street corners veiled women and bearded men and naked children and skulking dogs stared at them, and here and there came the clapping of hands and shouts of wonder at the sight of the Germans who had come to help the Turks win the war.

In Hodeida tent houses were quickly put up for the men of the *Emden*. The officers were given a house overlooking the town, from which they could see the French heavy cruiser offshore, making its very effective blockade of the port of Hodeida.

24. THE LONG MARCH

OR SEVERAL days they rested and saw the sights. The Turks would not hear of their leaving immediately and there was no opportunity to send messengers back to the *Choising*'s point of rendezvous. Von Mückc stood on the roof of his borrowed house on the second night and fired three shells from his signaling pistol, the agreed signal that there was grave danger in these waters and that the *Choising* must depart immediately for the neutral port of Massawa. With a heart that must have been much lightened to be away from the demands of the *Emden* party, Captain Minkiewitz steamed away, and eventually he reached the port of Massawa and safety from the enemies who overran those waters.

They left Hodeida on the Kaiser's birthday, but only after a celebration of the birthday and their honored presence. German and Turkish soldiers all formed in the middle of the town square, the Germans surrounded by Turks. Kapitän-leutnant von Mücke and the Turkish colonel reviewed the troops, and then von Mücke made a speech in German in honor of the Kaiser, and the German and Turkish troops all cheered. The Turkish colonel called for three cheers for the sultan, and the Germans and the Turks all cheered again.

The troops paraded and bands played, and all the men then marched back to the Turkish barracks for a feast of mutton and rice while the officers went to the palace of the mayor of Hodeida for a feast—mutton and rice. At five o'clock in the afternoon the party set out, the Germans all on horses and mules, their baggage carried by donkeys and camels.

Five o'clock was the proper hour. They would travel at night and sleep in the daytime under canvas. It was quite impossible to travel in the heat of the day. The Germans mounted their animals and the Turkish garrison formed a lane down which they passed, the bands playing again as they rode out toward the mountains of Yemen on a journey that would last three weeks.

An hour after leaving Hodeida the caravan was in the heart of the desert. There was no road, not even a trail; occasionally they saw the signs of a previous caravan, but as often as not these were covered by the blowing, drifting sand. All around them was sand, white and yellow sand, with a bit of dry grass tufting here and there.

In the beginning there were many stops, because the sailors kept falling from their mounts, or were thrown in a battle of wits with horse or mule. The officers could ride, for they had the benefit of the gentle life in Tsingtao behind them, but the men could not, and the officers spent much of that first evening chasing riderless animals and resaddling others. From this developed an unusual form for the caravan: The officers rode in the rear, reassembling the troops who had fallen and forming them into a rear guard. All the way this became the pattern.

It was wild and fierce country. The nights were clear and bright and sometimes cold, since the land did not hold the heat of the day. The caravan rode all night every night, stopping only two or three times for half an hour's rest.

No one had told them in Hodeida, for it was common knowledge and not a fig was given for it, that the region through which they must pass was the haunt of robbers and murderers. At the end of the first night of travel they had passed enough skeletons of animals *and men* so that they knew what their fate might be. On the second night out they had another reminder. Suddenly in the moonlight on the side of the road there appeared a dozen heavily armed men, bandoliers of ammunition about their shoulders, mounted on swift riding camels. The Turkish police who accompanied and guided the German war party said these were robbers, and the police advised the men to stop and bring up their arms. This was not difficult since every German was now armed to the teeth. The animals were stopped and the long noses of rifles began to train toward the sides of the ravine that formed a road at that point. The robbers saw that they had a band of heavily armed men to deal with, and they vanished among the dunes.

On the third night out the caravan left the flat desert country and moved into the mountains. These mountains rise almost straight out of the desert to eight thousand feet and more, and now the route was upward. As they rose they moved through narrow, twisting ravines and tumbling rocks in stream beds that were quite dry. But eventually they came out of this arid land and into farmland, fruited valleys and forested mountain sides, often topped by stone castles where the sheikhs lived in protection against the marauding bands of robbers.

The farther they traveled the more difficult the trip became. In the last few days before they reached the town of Menakha they crossed by a tortuous mountain trail, with sheer cliff on one side and sheer drop on the other, so steep that the men dismounted often and led their pack animals.

The mess squad and one officer traveled always ahead of the main party, starting a little before them in the evening and arriving at a camping point a few hours earlier, so that when the main body arrived the major meal of the day was ready for them to eat. Then they wriggled off to roll up in blankets and sleep.

Most of the stops were made at inns prepared by the Turkish army for the use of troops. Once in a while a camp was made elsewhere, but it was safest and most comfortable to use these official stopping points, and they were located one day's journey apart.

Menakha represented the attainment of the peaks to the Germans. Several hours before they reached the town they came upon the Turkish garrison, which had marched out to meet and greet them and accompany them in glory into the town. The people cheered and danced and chanted as they came by, and a crowd of white-cloaked civilians bounded ahead of them all the way.

The Germans spent two days in this mountaintop resort, and then began their trip downward. Now, wonder of wonders, there was a road, a real road and a broad one that could be compared with a European highway. The long nights in the saddle had made the men of the *Emden* into riders, and they could maintain a formation. They rode easily along the road, looking at the camels grazing along the roadsides and in the distance seeing bands of wild gazellelike creatures and sometimes baboons on the sides of the mountain passes.

Several days of travel brought them to a point where they could see Sana, the capital of Yemen, on the plain below them. Turkish troops rode out to the edge of the plateau when they saw the dust of their visitors. They had been apprised of the coming of the Germans, and they brought a horde of civilians and the garrison band, which had been practicing and played a fair rendition of *Deutschland über alles* to warm the hearts of their guests.

The Germans paraded proudly through the city in company with the Turkish troops, and bands of men and women stood on the sides of the road waving. Even the French consul, who was being detained by the Turks, stepped out on his balcony to watch the Germans pass and listen to the band playing German patriotic songs.

The welcome of the people and the Turkish troops was all that von Mücke could have hoped for, but the welcome of the country itself was not up to his expectations. He had been misled by the exuberance of his hosts in Hodeida, or the miserable climate of that place had done its work already, and the hard trip had helped with the job. Less than a week after their arrival in Sana eighty percent of von Mücke's men were down with fever. Had he been a hygienist, he would have known that the fever must have been contracted elsewhere, and his doctor should have known.

That was not the worst of it. Soon those whose fever was brought under control with quinine came down with colds or with stomach cramps from the rapid changes in temperature and the water.

For two weeks the party rested in Sana. Von Mücke took the time to learn something about the countryside and the city. He discovered that the city, divided into Turkish, Arab, and Jewish quarters, was built as a fortress, with the streets located so they could be swept by gunfire. Yemen was a wild and forbidding place, and only a decade before no Turks were allowed in Sana. They had laid siege to this city and starved it into submission then. They had not starved the countryside into surrender, however, and there were many Arabs outside Sana who would shoot at the sight of a fez or a Turkish uniform.

Von Mücke learned in his two weeks in Sana just how difficult the journey overland would be. They would be surrounded all the way by Bedouin tribes who could not be guaranteed to be friendly. The commander of the Turkish garrison here was much more forthright with his German ally than had been the colonel in Hodeida. The land was not pacified. Their safety could not be guaranteed, although if they wished to proceed the Turks would send troops with them on the journey.

The illness of his men and the dangers from climate and sickness as well as wild enemies were enough to bring pause to any man. The men continued to be sick, and that convinced von Mücke that it would not do to attempt the difficult overland journey. His men were sailors. He told the Turks to stop the preparations for the overland caravan. He would return to Hodeida, and he and his little force would take their chances of travel in the manner they knew best; they would go home by sea.

25. PERILOUS VOYAGE

ON MÜCKE searched the waterfront at Hodeida, under the nose of the French warship there, and discovered two small sailing boats, each about forty feet long and twelve feet wide, of the variety called zambuks along the Arabian shore. He purchased these in behalf of the German Navy, and had them sent north to the Bay of Yabana. It would never do to try to embark from Hodeida. He had been warned that spies must already have told the allies of the presence of a German war party in the area. Von Mücke listened to his informants and carefully made it public that he planned to sail from Isa Bay, a few miles away, on March 13. He intended no such thing. The day before he set watch on Isa Bay. It was not easy because there was no house or tree or brush to shelter men from the sand. But it *was* easy for von Mücke to observe the antics of the British gunboat which suddenly came into Isa Bay that evening, hunting up and down the shore by searchlight for Germans who were supposed to be encamped there waiting for the dawn.

173

Two days later, March 14, at five o'clock in the evening, Commodore von Mücke set sail from Yabana with his two-ship fleet. They had only one German war flag with them, and this was flown from the masthead of his "flagship." The sick were all aboard the second zambuk, and there were several of them, suffering from malaria, dysentery, and typhus.

Von Mücke chose a difficult course, quite purposefully; he steered along inside the Farsan Bank, which runs along the shore of the Arabian Peninsula for 350 miles. No ocean-going vessel would come near the bank, because it is guarded on the outside by a series of coral reefs, and even inside the waters are treacherous and filled with shallows. But here was safety of a sort.

Now the force numbered seventy men, including German-speaking Arabs who could translate for them, and the crews of the zambuks who were valuable to work the boats and also to appear when necessary to show the enemies of the Germans that these were Arab sailing craft. Each of the forty-foot vessels, then, carried thirty-five men crowded together. The days were extremely trying, and the men of the *Emden* stretched blankets across the ships from the bulwarks, in order to have some shade. They cooked at an open fireplace lined with tin, eating rice and mutton day after day. Occasionally they anchored at night, and one night they were given lodging by a pasha known to some of the Arabs of their crew. But at daybreak they were up again and in the boats, journeying northward.

The trip was extremely slow. The flat-bottomed boats made little headway, and the sails spilled much of the wind without getting full motive power from it. Worst of all was the frequency with which calms settled on the waters close inshore.

On March 17, Commodore von Mücke decided to anchor for the night, and to follow that practice thereafter. They were entering an area only vaguely charted on their maps, and the crews of their zambuks did not know the waters. It would not be safe to travel more in the darkness.

That evening they came near the island of Marka, von Mücke's zambuk leading and the other two hundred yards astern. Suddenly the lead boat struck a reef, pounded once, then again, but fell away. Von Mücke ordered the anchor dropped at once and began to examine the craft for damage. Fortunately it was not seriously hurt. Then he tried to signal the men in the second boat to sheer away from the reefs, and the captain of the second zambuk did avoid the reef they had struck, only to impale his boat on another. A flag was run up the masthead, showing that something was wrong, and in a moment von Mücke saw that was the matter. The second zambuk slowly disappeared from sight until only its masthead was showing.

It was just after six o'clock, but it was almost sundown, and near the equator the sun drops and nights set in within a few moments. Nor was there a moon to help them that night, so if they were to save boat or crew they must work quickly.

The anchor was hoisted, the sail was put up, and they moved back through the dangerous water to try to find their comrades. They had no small boats to send out—only a single dugout canoe, and now the sea was running high and the wind was brisker than they liked.

It grew dark suddenly, and von Mücke tried to light the single lantern his zambuk carried. He could not light it; each time he touched a match to the wick the wind blew it out. He had with him a few torches, and he called for them, but they would not light either; they had grown too damp in the months since they had been taken from the stores of the *Emden* for the fateful adventure on Direction Island.

Suddenly, although they were not quite sure where they were at that moment, they heard voices behind them, and discovered that the survivors from the zambuk had reached them and then swum past. Von Mücke shouted back. He was very worried, because this water was known to be heavily infested by sharks. He was worried, too, about the sick aboard the other boat. Had they been able to save themselves or had their comrades saved them?

No light could be made. Finally von Mücke piled firewood in the bottom of the boat, poured gasoline over it, and lighted a bonfire. This was a beacon; it also helped dry their torches until they would burn. He sent off some shots from his signaling pistol, even though these would be visible to any ship within two miles. The chance had to be taken if the party was to be kept together.

His little dugout was sent out, and soon it returned, followed by the dugout of the other zambuk. The men were found, clinging to the wreck or floundering in the water. Swimmers began to arrive alongside and to clamber in or be pulled in, thrashing in their life vests. Before long there were fifty people in the zambuk, and it was apparent that no more could climb in. But more men had to be brought in, almost twenty more. So the crew began jettisoning their belongings; provisions and water and personal treasures were thrown over the side until all that was left were the guns, ammunition, and enough food and water for only three days.

The lights lasted just long enough for the last officer to be rescued, then they were left in darkness.

Aboard the flagship, Leutnant Schmidt and the others told

their story. Their ship had been holed and had settled rapidly, but not so deeply that they could not remain aboard. They sounded around her and discovered that they lay on the edge of a reef, with a sharp dropoff into which their boat might fall given any twist of current or heavy wind. For the moment, however, they were safe until the flagship could rescue them.

Their plight had been noticed by another zambuk which had come into the lee of Marka Island, and a small boat had come to their rescue. Or so it seemed. The small boat had come alongside, and some rapid questions had been shouted in Arabic. Then the men in the boat had seen Dr. Lang's pith helmet and had shouted questions about the nationality of these people. The Arab crew had been forced to admit that these were Europeans, and the owners of the other zambuk swore that the infidel dogs could drown and turned away. They were members of the Idriss tribe, which hated Turks but hated Europeans more.

The next morning von Mücke sent an interpreter to the other zambuk offering a fortune if the captain would sell or even let them rent his ship for a few days. The captain spat and sent the interpreter back with a harsh message. Even if the Germans offered them a hundred thousand English pounds they would do nothing for them. They were infidel dogs and deserved to die.

Von Mücke considered the obvious course, which was to take the zambuk by force, but as he made those plans, dawn broke and with it came a following wind from the south. He could sail, even with his overloaded ship, in this weather, and it would be best not to arouse the Arabs by attacking some of their number if it could be avoided.

The men of the *Emden* moved to the wrecked zambuk,

which had tilted off into deeper water but had not yet fallen down the steep side of the reef. They dived and recovered the two machine guns that had been aboard her and some pistols, rifles, and ammunition. But their clothing and, most important, their medical supplies were lost beneath the tilted boat and could not be recovered.

The one blessing was the weather. In one afternoon they made as much mileage as they had made in the previous six days, and that very evening they arrived at the town of Kunfuda, a point almost halfway up the Arabian Peninsula. They rested for a few days at Kunfuda, entertained by local officials with feasts night after night. Von Mücke was fortunate enough to be introduced to a traveling Turkish official and his wife. They were seeking passage back to Constantinople and they were glad to join this band of armed men, for they were afraid of robbers and Bedouin tribesmen both on land and on sea. The official agreed to help von Mücke find another boat and to translate for him if they could come along. It was an admirable arrangement for all concerned.

Through the Turkish official's intervention, they were able to charter a large zambuk, one almost twice as large as their flagship, and they abandoned the old boat and took to the new, the entire landing party, with the Turkish official and his wife. Now they seemed to be out of difficulty. This ship sailed like a ship, and it had decent accommodations, at least for the officers and the civilians. There seemed to be no reason why they could not sail on and safely arrive at some port where they could take transportation to Constantinople.

All went well as far as El-Lith, a few miles north of Kunfuda. There they stopped for provisions and to learn the news. From this point on they would go into the open sea, for here was the end of the Farsan Bank that kept the foreign ships away from the Arab shore. It was fortunate that they stopped, for through the Turkish official they came into possession of a letter from a merchant in Jidda, the port to which they were next bound. The merchant wrote that Jidda was blockaded by the British and that no ship, not even a zambuk, was allowed to enter the harbor until after it was inspected by a British naval boarding party.

That was the end of the voyage of the men of the *Emden* in the Red Sea. Now Kapitänleutnant von Mücke knew he had no recourse but to travel overland, and he began looking for the animals and supplies he would need to take a camel caravan across the desert.

26. THE CARAVAN

IN TWO days von Mücke rounded up ninety camels. He purchased straw mats and food and water for the journey. He supervised the boiling of the water and the loading of the camels. He knew nothing about camels, but he made it his affair to learn, and in those two days he acquired a very fair knowledge of the art of loading and goading a recalcitrant ship of the desert.

On March 28 the men of the *Emden* set forth with their ninety camels and the promise that twenty more laden with supplies would meet them within a few days. The officers rode on free camels, but the riding camels of the men were fastened together by ropes, the muzzle of one camel tied to a rope four yards long that was then tied to the tail of the camel in front. This was slow going, but safe, for if the men had difficulty in learning to ride horses, they would have met tragedy in coping with riding camels in the heat of the desert.

Four days out from El-Lith, the party arrived at a well which was said to be just one day's march from Jidda, the party's next objective. Here the Turks from El-Lith left them, along with the sheikh of El-Lith, and they were greeted by an officer and seventeen Turkish policemen from Jidda—but no sheikh. The entire party lay down on straw mats and woolen blankets, pushing in as far as possible among the thorny desert plants to find protection from the blazing sun. Von Mücke and his officers supervised the cooking of the usual rice and mutton; he, now sporting a pink turban, walked smartly among the campfires, encouraging his men with a word or a pat on the shoulder here and there. He had grown more slender than ever and seemed taller and younger than his thirty-three years, in spite of the yellow beard that covered his brown face. The sharpness that had been part of his job as first officer of the *Emden* seemed to have disappeared; even with the added responsibility of command, he was making a better impression on his men as captain than he had as first officer. He was gentler, for one thing, made so by the sickness and death and the knowledge that these men—boys, most of them—were being asked to undertake the impossible.

At four o'clock in the afternoon the party struggled out of the sand and began to move ahead. The route now took them away from the Red Sea, inland among sand hills that undulated across the horizon, cutting visibility in any direction to around four hundred yards. The hills were covered with rough desert grass which grew here about two feet high.

Darkness came and the caravan continued to move forward. The moon came up and reflected brightly on the sand. Not long afterward there suddenly appeared a dozen Bedouins on horseback, who came out from behind a hill on the right and vanished down the trail which the caravan had just vacated. The police officers took tight hold of their guns. These were robbers, the Turkish commander told von

Mücke, probably part of a band of about forty who had been terrorizing caravans in the area during recent weeks.

Von Mücke did not become too concerned about forty bandits, since his party consisted of nearly seventy armed men, including the police. Still, he was careful. He divided his camels into two lines of fifty, and he and his officers examined every man's gun and warned each man against going to sleep on his camel.

All was quiet that night, except for the soft clopping of the camels in the sand as they moved at their jolting trot across the desert. At dawn von Mücke began to relax again; it was common knowledge that the Bedouins never attacked in the daytime. He slung his rifle across his saddle, took the heavy cartridge belt off his waist, and began to ride back down the line from the front to check his men.

Suddenly, as he reached the midpoint of the caravan, he heard a loud whistle, a signal, followed immediately by a volley of rifle fire that came from all directions. They were ambushed, caught between the dunes on the left and ahead, and the foothills of a range of mountains on the right. From cover on every side the Arab bandits were firing down on the caravan.

Von Mücke leaped off his camel, grabbing his rifle as he ran, and shouted for his men to follow him to the head of the caravan, where the firing seemed heaviest. As he moved up he could see that the enemy was about eighty yards away. He could see very little more but he was comforted because neither could the raiders. The men were on the ground; the bandits were firing at flashes and at the silhouettes of the camels.

Von Mücke now began to dispose his force. Some men were sent back to reinforce the rear guard. The important task, however, was to bring out the machine guns, which would give the caravan an infinite superiority of firepower. Two of these guns were strapped to the backs of camels at the head of the column and two were at the rear. In a few minutes all four guns were out and trained. In the front, von Mücke ordered his gunners to fire a few bursts and when this was done suddenly the desert became quiet. The raiders had not expected their victims to be so heavily armed.

During the lull of the next few minutes von Mücke and his officers brought the men into a concentration at the left front, where the fire had been heaviest and where he supposed the most of the raiders were hidden. The camels were pulled in and made to lie down so they would not provide such outstanding targets. The officers were assigned to small details of men.

As the sun began to come over the horizon, they could see their enemy. The sand hills were dotted with black and gray figures; von Mücke estimated that there must be at least three hundred Arabs around them.

They waited uncomfortably. One young sailor on the right asked permission to ask a question. Von Mücke assented. The sailor wanted to know how soon they were going to charge the enemy with their bayonets.

Von Mücke did not hesitate. Under the cover of the machine guns, the men with rifles charged out, first to the left, then to the right. The Bedouins faded away before them, falling back rather than engaging in hand-to-hand combat.

Another charge and they had enlarged the circle of their perimeter to about 1,200 yards. This was more comfortable. The machine guns were spread out, each to cover a section of the perimeter, and the party sat down to wait. The enemy had backed away and firing had stopped again completely.

Von Mücke stopped to count noses. Only one German sailor was wounded, but all the policemen had vanished except seven, and among their Arab camel drivers, nearly all were either dead or wounded.

Looking around, outside their perimeter, they found fifteen dead Bedouins but were able to recover only one enemy rifle, a British gun of the most modern type.

The Arabs had moved off to distant sand hills out of respect for the machine guns and bayonets, but they were still there in force, waiting in the sun. The heat of day was approaching, and the caravan could not remain long in the sun without shelter. Von Mücke decided to move.

A third of the camels were dead or injured. They were stripped of necessities, and the sound camels were loaded with only necessities. Von Mücke abandoned the camel caravan route and turned left to find the sea, intending to follow its shores so that at least he would have flank protection on one side.

The caravan was now divided into six lines of camels which traveled abreast. The wounded Arabs and the one German sailor were strapped to camels so that they hung on the inside flanks of the beasts and were protected from bullets by the animals. Two camels bearing machine guns were put at the head of the column and two brought up the rear. Now twenty men were detached from the column. Ten, under officers, were sent out forward on their camels as skirmishers, and ten dropped back 150 yards to form a rear guard.

Except for nine men, this disposition exhausted the supply of rifles. The nine were split, five on one side and four on the other, and they became flank guards. The pistols were allocated to the other men, who would ride in the main body of the caravan. They would not carry far but they would be valuable in close combat. Leutnant Gerdts took the advance guard, Leutnant Schmidt took the rear guard, Leutnant Gyssling was in charge of the flankers, and Leutnant Wellman and the doctor remained with the caravan itself.

The caravan set forth again, this time flying the German flag and banner. If there were any mistake on the part of the attackers, this was their opportunity to remedy it. There was no mistake. Ten minutes later the fire began again. The Arabs were riding on all sides of them, out of sight, and stopping to ascend a sand mound and fire off a few harrying shots. The shots came from every direction, but they were concentrated in the rear. From Leutnant Schmidt's area came constant sounds of fire, and on going back, Von Mücke learned that Schmidt and his men were forced to stop every few hundred yards to return the enemy fire. When they did so, the enemy faded away, only to reappear in another position in five minutes.

Von Mücke was investigating this rear-guard problem when the enemy increased their activity suddenly. One of the machine gun camels fell, and Leutnant Schmidt stopped the rear guard to protect the gun while it was taken off the dead camel and repacked on a live one. Just then von Mücke was called to the front, where Leutnant Gerdts was in trouble. The whole area ahead was dotted with figures, and the rate of fire was increasing. The attack was being launched again.

Von Mücke arrived at the front, pursued by a sailor, who reported the events in the rear guard. Firing had increased there, too.

Von Mücke could hear it. From the rear the two machine guns were firing. He gave the signal to stop the caravan. Now

all the Arab drivers who could move ran away to join the
Bedouins and the other camel drivers, and the Germans and
their few police companions were left alone. It was not easy
to stop the caravan and force the camels to lie down, but the
officers had seen von Mücke do it, and they now pushed and
pulled to bring the caravan to some kind of unity in a protected position.

Von Mücke moved to the rear guard to see what was happening, afoot now, having forced his camel to lie on the
ground. He found one seaman, Rademacher, dead on the
ground, and Leutnant Schmidt shot through the chest and
through the abdomen. Either wound was fatal. He was lying,
conscious and gasping, on the ground.

As von Mücke looked around the perimeter, Leutnant
Wellman came up with two camels to retrieve the machine
guns, and he was placed in charge of the rear guard.

Suddenly the firing stopped and von Mücke looked up to
see two of their remaining Arab policemen running toward
the Bedouins, carrying large white flags. Another said they
had gone to parley with the enemy.

Von Mücke realized now that it was an enemy, and not
robbers as he had believed. He had no faith in talk, but the
knowledge that this was an organized force changed his
course of action. He decided to fortify his position as best he
could and remain where he was, awaiting help. Thus the
machine guns could be used for protection. It was simply a
question of how long they could hold out and how long it
would be before a relieving force arrived, bringing water,
food, and ammunition.

The Turkish official, one of those wounded in the leg, took
his wife and went to join the police in the parley with the
Arabs.

The men were put to work digging in the sand. The camels were unsaddled and moved to a central point, to become the hub of the defense. The saddles were filled with sand and dotted about the perimeter to make a rampart. Between them sacks of rice and coffee and other provisions were piled, and sand was heaped around to make a wall. The bottles containing the precious water were buried in the sand where they would be as safe as possible from gunfire. Inside the perimeter another rampart was made, about four feet high, constructed of empty petroleum cans filled with sand. This was to be the hospital. Leutnant Schmidt could be carried there to join the wounded German soldier and the wounded Arabs. Dr. Lang presided over this makeshift infirmary.

The lull lasted for some time. There was time to bury seaman Rademacher and to make a stretcher to transport Leutnant Schmidt. The four machine guns were set up at the edges of the perimeter, and the riflemen were scattered between them.

The preparations were all made when the Arab policemen returned from their parley with the Bedouin leaders, bearing conditions for a truce. The Germans were to give up all their arms and ammunition, to surrender their camels and their food and water. If they would sign a note on their government to pay eleven thousand gold pounds to the Bedouins, then they would be allowed to go in peace. The Turkish official did not return.

Von Mücke was quite certain that if they gave up their arms they would be massacred, or at the very least imprisoned and held for ransom. He had no intention of surrendering, and he said so, whereupon the firing began again.

27. THE SIEGE

KAPITÄNLEUTNANT VON MÜCKE knew that the German position was extremely perilous. They were short of ammunition, and even shorter of dependable ammunition. When the firing began again he broke into some of the extra ammunition that had been carried on the second zambuk, had been sunk, and had been rescued. Several riflemen reported that some of the cartridges would not fire. Von Mücke gathered up the good ammunition then and distributed it carefully among the machine guns. A rifleman could eject a bad cartridge and replace it quickly. The jamming of a machine gun at this point might be fatal.

From the sand hills the Bedouins continued firing, sometimes heavily, sometimes lightly, until darkness. They made no attempt to rush the German position, warned away by the ugly snouts of the Maxim guns.

Inside the perimeter, von Mücke and his men prepared to resist a night attack. The firing had not caused any more casualties, except among the camels, and von Mücke was not concerned about them; a dead camel was probably better protection against gunfire than a live one, until the decay set in.

All day the Germans kept flat behind their ramparts. If a man raised his head he drew fire. Under these circumstances there was little movement; only von Mücke crawled about the sand, checking his defenses and speaking to his men.

The logical time for an enemy charge was the few minutes after sunset before the moon began to rise. Then darkness was so black that the defenders could scarcely see their ramparts and nothing beyond them was visible. They were ready and waiting nervously for the whistle's sound, the shots, and the yells of charging tribesmen, but out in the blackness nothing stirred.

When the moon came up, von Mücke could see some three hundred yards outside their position. Lookouts were posted so they would not be surprised, and then he set the men to work to improve the tiny fortress. First the dead camels had to be removed. In the heat of the day they had already begun to stink, and by the next day they would be unbearable. They were dragged out to the south of the perimeter, since the prevailing wind at this season was from the north.

Water was served out in careful rations and hardtack was broken out from one of the cases and given out to the men. Now trenches were made around the perimeter so the men could move a little and would not be forced to crawl along the ground.

At nine o'clock, Leutnant Schmidt died. Von Mücke ordered the men to dig a grave as deep as possible in the center of the perimeter, and he and the other officers carried their comrade to it. There was no sewing in a sack, no burial service, no volley of fire over the grave. They could not waste their ammunition on the dead.

By midnight the trenches had been deepened, the perimeter strengthened, and the wounded cared for. It should have been time for rest. But not for Kapitänleutnant von Mücke. He made his way slowly around the camp, checking each man's gun and helping clean and test it. The machine guns were gone over. The men wrapped their handkerchiefs around the firing mechanisms and stuffed cloth into the muzzles to keep the sand out. Then he set up watches, as on shipboard. Half the men would sleep while the others stayed on guard. Always at least one officer was awake and touring the perimeter.

The men slept with their guns in their hands that night, but there was no attack. Von Mücke slept hardly at all. Late that night when the moon had gone down, he dispatched a man for assistance. It was not a German, for the chances of a German making his way to Jidda through the lines were so slim as to be negligible. The messenger was an Arab, one von Mücke was inclined to trust because he had served the Germans as interpreter and handyman all the way from Hodeida.

Half an hour before sunrise, von Mücke awakened his men. If there was to be an attack that morning it would come with dawn. He proposed, if the enemy began to fire, to return it with such vigor that the Arabs would overestimate their supply of ammunition and would remain wary. He estimated that it was about ten hours to Jidda and that if the messenger got through, they should be able to expect relief that night or the next morning. Now it was a problem of holding out. If the messenger had not gotten through, it was still a problem of holding out.

Von Mücke had been correct in his estimate of the enemy's intentions. As dawn broke and the sun came up suddenly behind the hills, a volley of fire broke out all around the camp, and a wave of firing followed it. The Germans fired back at every head that appeared and the machine guns fired a few bursts. If they were short bursts, that information did not seem to mean anything to the Arabs.

The shooting died down quickly, and during the morning shots were fired only when there was movement in the camp.

As the sun rose and began to beat down in its desert ferocity, the men lay in their trenches, seeking what shelter they could from the parapet and shirts thrown up around their heads.

Just before the morning attack each man had a drink of water and was given a handful of hardtack. He would have no other food or water until night fell; there was no way of moving outside the trenches without exposing men to fire. The Germans learned that early in the day when two of the seamen became careless and exposed themselves. Both were wounded in the body, and the officers moved out to rescue them and drag them into the inner enclosure.

That afternoon, as the men of the *Emden* lay in the heat, fighting sand and black beetles that overran their camp in search of food and camel dung, von Mücke could look across to the sea and watch peculiar activity there. He saw two zambuks pulled in to shore and from them an unending stream of Arabs carrying provisions back and forth. Far out in the desert he could also see camels grazing. So some of his enemies had come by sea and some by land, and they were prepared for a long siege. He estimated the enemy force now at eight hundred men.

He was not prepared for siege. The wounded were suffering terribly. All the medicines of the party had gone down in that second zambuk; all that remained were the emergency dressings the men carried in their kits and a few bottles of brandy for anesthetic.

The heat was sapping and dangerous. The men burned their hands on the barrels of their rifles. They could not wear the headcloths they had adopted from the Arabs, because the colors were bright and would bring enemy fire. Von Mücke took off his pink turban, and his head ached and his eyes swam in the sun.

It grew so hot that the grease-soaked camel saddles around the perimeter began to smoke and threatened to burst into flame before the men doused them with hot sand.

The sand drifted in the wind and the men were put to work repairing the trenches. The sand got into their eyes and made them red from weeping. It caked their nostrils and cracked their lips and rubbed their faces raw. The sweat got into the cracks and their lips and faces swelled and turned red and gray.

All afternoon vultures circled the camp, attracted by the smell from the rotting camel meat. Their presence was unnerving, but they did not dare to land.

As darkness fell and the expected attack again did not materialize in the dangerous hour after sunset, von Mücke's confidence wavered. What if the messenger he had sent had defected to the enemy? He dispatched two more Arabs—two of the remaining police, who tore up their uniforms and managed to look as much like Bedouins as possible. He counted the hours. Ten hours to Jidda, ten hours back, and half a day to prepare for the fight. If the man had gotten through, relief could be expected that night.

No relief came. The men slept and guarded in shifts. At

midnight the sleepers were aroused by shots, and von Mücke crept to the guard post from which they had come.

"Where are they?" he said.

"Straight ahead," said the guard. "There goes one now."

He fired at a slinking shape about forty yards from the perimeter. Von Mücke strained his eyes in the night. Soon he could see that the shape had four legs and a tail. It was a jackal, making a meal from one of the camels.

That night one of the wounded died.

As dawn broke the next morning, von Mücke took stock. This would be the last day. By nightfall they would have exhausted their strength, and any amount of rationing of water and food could only spell disaster after that. They faced an enemy who was well supplied from the sea, who obviously had plenty of water and food and ammunition. They had only two chances. The relief column would come, or they must fight their way out and try to make it to Jidda by night.

He moved among the officers and the men giving his instructions. They were to stay in the position all day, conserving their strength and ammunition. When darkness fell, they were to force their way through to Jidda. The sick and wounded would have to be deserted; only thus could any of them hope to survive.

Around noon of this third day an Arab appeared on the hill before them waving a white flag and von Mücke beckoned him in. The Bedouin leaders had reduced their demands, the messenger said. They would settle now for promise of payment of twenty-two thousand pounds in gold. The Germans could keep their arms and ammunition and food and water.

Although his arms were few, his ammunition nearly exhausted, his water gone except for a drink for each man that evening, and his food reduced to rice and hardtack, von Mücke pretended that the caravan could hold out for weeks. He pointed to a stack of empty cans and said he was indicating part of their water supply. As for ammunition, it was only because of Christian charity that they had not descended on the Arabs with the machine guns and wiped them out. No, he said, they would not accept the offer. The Arabs could go back and fight some more.

Von Mücke reasoned that the Arabs would not be coming to him if they did not know something was happening. He hoped the word had gotten through to Jidda and that the relief column was on its way. He could not tell.

So von Mücke stalled.

The emissary went back with his high-flown statements, to return in half an hour and repeat the original offer. Von Mücke said he wanted to talk to their leader. The envoy returned to the Arab lines and came back a second time to report that if the Germans did not agree at once to the terms there would be plenty of fighting. Von Mücke said there had already been plenty of fighting and the dispirited negotiator went away.

In a few moments the camp rang with shots. The Arab fire was heavier than it had been at any time since the beginning of the siege. Then, suddenly, it stopped. A quarter of an hour passed and there was not a sound. Another fifteen minutes went by, and von Mücke cautiously raised his head. The horizon was empty. The zambuks were gone. No camels stood grazing on the hills; there were no camels about at all except their few mangy live ones and the evil-smelling dead ones around the perimeter.

Soon he arose cautiously. There was no fire. The others arose. Still the air was silent. They sent out searchers. The Arabs were gone, every camel, every robe, every gun of them.

The men were anxious to be off, even on foot, with the camels left to carry the wounded, but von Mücke would not move by day. It might be a ruse, and the enemy might be lurking beyond the next hill. In any event he would not travel until nightfall.

An hour went by, then in the distance two figures on camelback appeared, carrying a white flag. They dismounted and identified themselves as representatives of the ruler of Mecca, who had heard of the attack on the Germans and had sent troops to relieve them.

Von Mücke scarcely believed them. He had approached the parley with cocked pistol and drawn sword and he did not put them down. The Arabs seemed to understand his disbelief, but quite comfortably they reassured him. Abdullah, second son of the ruler, would soon appear leading the relief and they would see. It was true; in half an hour along came a troop of some seventy camel-borne soldiers, carrying a red banner marked in Arabic. It bore verses from the Koran, the interpreter said. The Arabs were chanting and some of them were beating on drums as they came.

Prince Abdullah rode up to the gathering and presented his father's greeting and apologies for the attack by the Bedouins. Now they could go to Jidda in peace, and Abdullah and his troops would accompany them.

It took the Europeans some time, with the help of the Meccan soldiers, to round up the camels, saddle them, and get the caravan's supplies loaded again. Many supplies had to be left behind, because forty of the camels had been shot.

Late in the afternoon they were ready to go, and they began to march, accompanied by Abdullah and his men. At evening they came to an oasis and there they stopped. Von Mücke wanted his men to wash and clean up before appearing in Jidda. They camped at the oasis, and the next morning they rode in dignity into the city.

28. THE LAST LAP

A T JIDDA the wounded were placed in a clean Turkish military hospital and Kapitänleutnant von Mücke rested with his men for a few days, considering again the best manner in which they might make their way to the railroad. In spite of the strenuous adventures of the last week, they had come only a few miles and were nearly as far as ever away from the railroad to Constantinople and Berlin.

He purchased a new large zambuk in the name of His Imperial Majesty and hired an experienced pilot and crew.

He borrowed a motor launch and each day scoured the harbor, trying to ascertain the pattern followed by the British in their blockade. On the night of April 8 the wounded were taken from the hospital, with the assurance of Dr. Lang that they were fit for travel, at least by ship, and the zambuk was loaded and set to sea. The wind held steady all night long and by daybreak they were well away from the coast of Jidda, hugging the shoreline far north, creeping behind the reefs.

It was a most uneventful voyage. They passed a few fishing boats and some coastal zambuks traveling southward, but saw no British ship or other sign of Europeans, and on April 28 they arrived at Sherm Munnaiburra, a tiny bay south of El-Wegh, the town inland where they would head by camel caravan toward the railroad at El-Ala. This decision was made almost on a moment's notice: von Mücke somehow felt uneasy about continuing the sea voyage, and, leaving their provisions aboard the zambuk, they found camels and began the overland trip.

On April 29 they found enough camels in El-Wegh to begin the trek to the railroad. They bathed in El-Wegh, and changed their clothing, dressing more or less as they would out of sheer need. Most of them had lost their campaign hats with the red, white, and black cockades. Their shirts and trousers had been torn and wrecked in the shipwreck and the siege. They found other clothing; some wore fezzes, some wore Arab headcloths, and von Mücke retained his pink turban.

On May 2, 1915, at eight o'clock in the morning, the men of the *Emden* boarded their camels and set forth for the railhead.

The men were familiar enough now with camels that they could safely follow the custom of this northern country and guide their own mounts without being tied together in caravan. Von Mücke rode on ahead of the caravan to reach the station at El-Ala and order a train for his men. They arrived at noon to find a special train waiting.

When the men arrived a few hours later, von Mücke formed them on the edge of the village into a marching unit and they came smartly, their battle flags flying, up to the train. In a few moments it started, and began carrying them homeward at the rate of twenty miles an hour.

By rail they traveled to Damascus and Aleppo, then across Asia Minor to Constantinople. The train stopped often and there were many gifts. There were new naval uniforms, sent from His Majesty's Ship *Breslau;* there were presents and messages, including word from the Kaiser himself that they had been awarded the Iron Cross. Von Mücke was given the Iron Cross first class for his exploits, plus the Saxon Johanniter order and the Bavarian Cross. He blushed in pleasure as he read the formal notices. Leutnant Gyssling, too, received the Bavarian Cross.

Von Mücke sent telegrams along the way. His first was to the German high naval command, asking for a new ship so he could fight against the enemy. His second was to his mother and father in Saxony, announcing his safe arrival in friendly lands.

On the train that first night, the officers and men celebrated with champagne and brandy.

The train trip to Constantinople took seventeen days. Every day there were stops and the local officials came out to greet the heroes and pay them homage. They changed from a Turkish to a German train at Damascus, which meant they had sleeping cars and sheets.

It was pomp and circumstance all the way, from a military parade during the changing of the trains at Damascus to receptions by the governors of the various Turkish provinces through which they passed. All the way von Mücke continued to shepherd his charges, although it was no longer strictly necessary.

He continued his chalk talks, giving his men the news of

the war, and in Baalbek he took the men on a tour of the Roman ruins and guided them like an expert. In Aleppo, when the official mail was received, he announced that all of them had the Iron Cross, and he read aloud to all of them the various messages of praise and endearment received from the fatherland.

Finally the train reached Haidar Pasha, the end of the railway, and there the men of the *Emden* were greeted by the first German naval officers they had since leaving their ship at Direction Island. Admiral Souchon, chief of the Mediterranean division for the Imperial Navy, was there with his staff in their blue-and-gold uniforms, waiting at the station. The men of the *Emden* stepped off their train in their shining new uniforms and lined up briskly. Kapitän-leutnant Hellmuth von Mücke stepped out in front of them and ordered a salute; on the right flank the flags of a German warship flew. He called his crew to attention, gave the salute, and lowered his sword, stepping toward his smiling admiral, and spoke huskily.

"I report the landing squad from the *Emden,* five officers, seven petty officers, and thirty men strong."